Army and Na
Londo

D0585914

At the Launch,
Saturday,
2nd. December 1989

Francis Salvesen.
283/500

Signed Limited Edition.

A Student at Arms

Francis Salvesen

Warrior Enterprises

First published for Warrior Enterprises in 1989
by White Tree Books, 49 Park St., Bristol.

Text and illustrations © 1989 Francis Salvesen
Photographs © Francis Salvesen and by kind permission of the Directorate
of Public Relations (Army) and Jim Farrar.

The characters and situations in this book are entirely true, and relate to real
people still alive and real situations, though one or two of the characters'
names have been disguised and most characters are addressed by their
Christian or nicknames.

This book is published with the approval of The Ministry of Defence
Directorate of Public Relations (Army). The views expressed are those of
the author and do not necessarily conform with official policy.

ISBN 0 948 265 19 1

Typeset by The Picador Group, Bristol
Printed and bound in Great Britain for Warrior Enterprises, Editorial Office:
Spruce House, 38 Kingswood Road, London SW2 4JH.
By WBC Ltd, Bristol and Maesteg.

CONTENTS

TO MY BROTHER OFFICERS

"To know one's limitations is a mark of wisdom; to rest content with them merits contempt." (Donald Hankey, *A Book of Wisdom*)

> "There is in all men, even the basest, some kinship with the Divine, something which is capable of rising superior to common passions and the lure of easy reward, superior to pain and loss, superior even to death. The true leader evokes this...The task of leadership is not to put greatness into humanity, but to elicit it, for greatness is there already." (John Buchan)

ACKNOWLEDGEMENTS

I acknowledge all the unswerving support and help I have received from so many friends and professionals in writing this book and wish to thank them:

Jonathan and Vanessa Minns, for encouraging me;

Major General Cooper, Commandant, The Royal Military Academy Sandhurst, for his endorsement;

Captain Barry (Directorate of Public Relations (Army), for permission to publish and for the supply of useful material;

Peter Townend (Tatler), for his words on 'The Commissioning Ball';

Crispin Swayne (Blues and Royals) for his witty reminiscences;

Colonel Robert Watson OBE (Royal Scots) for his military guidance;

The Very Rev.Dr R.Selby Wright CVO,DD,FRSE ('Uncle Ronnie'), my mentor;

My parents, Robin and Sari Salvesen, for being there;

Grania Mackey (Cambridge University) for her critique;

Mandy Foreman, for her advice on publishing;

Victoria Acland, for her advice on printing;

Dana Shaul, for her inspiration;

Major Donald Scott MBE (Royal Highland Fusiliers), for seeing the sparks of humour and bringing them to light in illustration;

Alice and Malcolm Liddell-Grainger, for their entertaining anecdotes;

Christopher Gunn Fowler (Queen's Own Highlanders) and Dominic Tayler (Royal Scots Dragoon Guards), for volunteering to find it all out for themselves!

The Committee of The Warriors Ball;

And to all those unsung heroes who continue to provide the British Army with 'Officers and Gentlemen' and the British People with our Freedom and Dignity.

"Everything is froth and bubble,
Two things stand like stone:
Help in someone else's trouble;
Courage in your own." (Crispin Swayne, Blues and Royals)

5

FOREWORD

"Ten good soldiers wisely led will beat
a hundred without a head" - Euripides

The author, in his letter asking me to write an introductory foreword to this book on Sandhurst, said that he hoped the book "will add a much needed breath of truth to the mountains of fable that grow from outside perceptions of the Academy". I would echo that sentiment wholeheartedly.

Officers have been trained at Sandhurst since 1811 and from that date the Academy has established for itself a name of considerable reknown as one of the foremost officer training academies in the world. Indeed many would claim that the Royal Military Academy has the highest reputation for excellence of any officer training establishment anywhere. Today anyone aspiring to a commission in the British Army, whether man of woman, career or short-service, regular or territorial under the age of 29 years, must pass through its gates if they are to achieve their ambition. To this number of citizens from the United Kingdom should be added those from over 70 overseas nations who have been sent by their countries to be taught the skills and qualities of an officer with their British contemporaries.

As perhaps the first post-war Commandant not trained at the Academy I began my first day with much trepidation and some slight understanding of the feelings of the young men and women arriving on their first day clutching their possessions from suitcase to ironing board wondering how on earth they will cope with the mysteries which surround Sandhurst. Like any great institution there is more myth than fact in the stories emanating from the Academy. Many are told with a hint of exaggeration by former cadets to heighten the nervousness of the newcomer.

The RMA motto is 'Serve To Lead' and that short phrase embodies the principle that it is a privilege to lead soldiers, a privilege which demands not only an excellent knowledge of one's job but also a desire to serve those men and women one is lucky enough to command both on and off duty. Sandhurst aims for excellence and it demands of the individual more than perhaps he or she has had to produce in the past. It asks for effort and enthusiasm throughout the training whether the subject is an individual's forte or not. It is here that the measure of individual quality so often lies. It is not that the person is brilliant at a particular subject or finds it easy but that he or she is prepared to give of their best and help those less gifted.

Great store is set by the qualities of leadership, written about so often by great leaders of the past:- courage, moral as well as physical, integrity, selflessness, enthusiasm and so on, and it is the Academy's aim to show its students why these qualities are as valuable today and to try and help them enhance and build on their own virtues for the benefit of their soldiers.

No foreword on Sandhurst would be complete without mention of the instructors. The young officer platoon commanders are the very best that the Army can provide. The Warrant and Non-Commissioned Officers, probably more well known to the uninitiated and more feared than anyone, are drawn from across the Army. Their reputation is second to none and to all those who in their first week give cause to be reprimanded, dare I say shouted at, by one of these redoubtable men, let me say, categorically, that they will teach you more about the soldiers you will lead, about the army you have joined, about the standards you must set than anyone else. The man remembered before all others for the rest of an officer's life is his platoon instructor. Throughout my time at the Academy my respect for this very special breed of soldier grew day by day as I understood more and more the skill with which he handled each different individual and the time he gave to help each one to gain the knowledge necessary to pass out.

Sandhurst has much to offer the potential officer which can not be quantified by the Ministry of Defence's laid down training objectives but which stem from its traditions, its people, its buildings and its general atmosphere. I would not pretend that it is an easy course or that every moment, particularly the struggle of the first five weeks, is fun. I am however quite sure that once set on the road to a commission there is no finer training, no better instructor and no greater sense of achievement to be found than at the Academy. Old fashioned values are sought; old fashioned methods are not. The student is taken from raw recruit to commissioned officer in a graduated manner with greater responsibility for himself and his colleagues being earned by time and merit. Sandhurst is not frightened of change but is an institution which constantly evolves round the firm principles of excellence, high standards and sound leadership.

My advice to any young man or woman about to enter a military career as an officer at Sandhurst is: take all the stories with a pinch of salt; go with a positive attitude and open mind; don't get depressed when things seem hard and do not always go your way; enjoy it and above all listen to your platoon Colour Sergeant.

Major General S. C. Cooper, Commandant,
The Royal Military Academy Sandhurst, June 1987 - April 1989

INTRODUCTION

"What do you *do* at Sandhurst?"

The question echoes resonantly from party to party unleashing a wealth of incipient adventures, which would make the 'Sun' look bland! These, like 'the attraction of the uniform', stir the imaginations of hosts of civilian peers. The aura of the Royal Military Academy hangs in the air, a reminder of our Imperial heritage, generating respect and adulation. The year at Sandhurst that transforms generations of students into the prestigious, world-acclaimed ranks of the British Officer Corps (and into the Officer Corps of Great Britain's allies) has always been an enigma - and will remain so. I hope in this book, however, to throw some light on the events that happen at Sandhurst, through an account of my own experiences. These will show how Sandhurst moulds so many students of different ages, backgrounds, religions, creeds and cultures with the characteristics that typify The British Army Officer.

'To show that you can express yourself in written English' is the official reason why year after year Officer Cadets at The Royal Military Academy Sandhurst sum up every week's training in journals. Once a month these journals are marked by the Platoon Commander, a Captain, who corrects the English, grades the content and returns the journals for the next few weeks of writing. The grades given affect the overall performance rating of each Officer Cadet; a bad 'Not Satisfactory' grade will result in a re-write, while a good grade pushes up the overall average. At the end of the year of training the best journals are collected in and read through by the Commandant, who awards a prize to the author of the journal which 'best represents the Military Life of an Officer Cadet'.

My Military Life has taken me through many adventures, from Armoured Infantry Warfare in Canada to frost-bitten exercises in the Northern Plains of West Germany. From my cadet training at Fettes until I resigned my Commission in 1988 I always carried with me a book called 'The Beloved Captain' by Donald Hankey. Given to me in 1982 by the Very Rev. Dr.R.Selby Wright (known to many Old Fettesians as 'Uncle Ronnie'), this collection of well-thumbed essays has inspired me throughout my army life. The aspirations of being an Officer and Gentleman are as fresh today as they were forty years ago: "After all, the virtues of a gentleman are Christian virtues—absence of selfishness, consideration for others, contempt of public opinion and honour before life". It was while in the army that Donald Hankey wrote articles for 'The Spectator' under the name of 'A Student in Arms', from which the title of my Journal is derived, arguing throughout that what matters most is the right sort of leader:

"For a few days he just watched. Then he started work. He picked out some of the most awkward ones, and, accompanied by a corporal, marched them away by themselves. Ingenuously he explained that he did not know much himself yet; but he thought that they might get on better if they drilled by themselves a bit, and that if he helped them, and they helped him, they would soon learn. His confidence was infectious. He looked at them, and they looked at him, and the men pulled themselves together and determined to do their best. Their best surprised themselves. His patience was inexhaustible. His simplicity could not fail to be understood. His keenness and optimism carried all with them. Very soon the awkward squad found themselves awkward no longer; and soon after that they ceased to be a squad and went back to the platoon.

Then he started to drill the platoon, with the sergeant standing by to point out his mistakes. Of course he made mistakes, and when that happened he never minded admitting it. He would explain what mistakes he had made, and try again. The result was that we began to take almost as much interest and pride in his progress as he did in ours. We were his men, and he was our leader. We felt that he was a credit to us, and we resolved to be a credit to him. There was a bond of mutual confidence and affection between us, which grew stronger and stronger as the months passed. He had a smile for almost every one; but we thought that he had a different smile for us."

"To know one's limitations is a mark of wisdom; to rest content with them merits contempt" . . .

I have tried to relate throughout the important and entertaining events of my life at Sandhurst as accurately as possible and in chronological order, as they occurred in my journal, removing only the mundane and tactical information. The content has been given the official sanction of The Directorate of Public Relations (Army), but I would like to emphasise that the views expressed within are my own and do not necessarily conform with official policy.

Francis R.C. Salvesen.

CHAPTER ONE: THE SCRUTINY BOARD

For most Officer Cadets entering the Royal Military Academy Sandhurst, the greatest accomplishment of our lives was to pass the Regular Commissions Board at Westbury. Without this success none of us would have even entered Sandhurst, let alone been Commissioned. Few forget the experience of those three and a half days of gruelling assessment and of the eight hundred or so that pass each year, few drop out of Sandhurst. My three and a half days began at Westbury Station on a wintry Monday morning in December, following a train journey from London, where I was met by a nonplussed Sergeant and ushered into the awaiting army minibus.

At eleven o'clock, having dropped off my case in my assigned bedroom, I was sitting in nervous anticipation of the introductory talk of the supervising officer. Around me sat fifty or so similarly awed potential Officers, nervously twitching. The Colonel walked in and the introduction began.

The written tests which followed the Colonel's talk provided a challenging but relatively easy initiation, as I had researched the likely general knowledge areas over the preceding week, knew most of the Service knowledge from school cadet training and was sufficiently up to date on current affairs. The essay was quite easy too, as we were given a wide range of subjects from which to choose and had three quarters of an hour in which to write it. Then the real fun began; the intelligence tests. The first of these involved picking the odd shape or number out from a series; the second was mathematical and as each of the three tests had been sampled beforehand, in an organised preview, I knew what I was on about and actually started to enjoy myself!

The remainder of our first day of mental stress was taken up with administration and documentation. My group of eight went back to our rooms after the documentation to discuss what was in front of us, though alienated by personal competitive suspicion; on average only half of us were to pass and it might be that one weak individual would let the rest of us down in the team tasks. We managed, with an injection of humour, to convince each other that we would all pass and moved through to the Mess for dinner. Our 'intake' had two female groups, whose accommodation was protected by "the roughest female Sergeant Major you've ever seen!" the girls informed us. Having had a confident start to the Board, I decided that wine was a prerequisite for our meal and, together with two members of my group, collected the chosen 'duty frees' from the bar and arranged one of the tables, inviting some of the girls to join us. The range of experience and military knowledge was immense. Some of the group had family connections, but, when asked, most drummed off well rehearsed arguments for why they should want to join the army as if I was interviewing them. I could see that the interviewers' task would have been greatly complicated by having to distinguish between reasons given parrot-fashion and honest expectations. I too had thought out most of the questions that I would be asked in the interviews and was intrigued by one jocular individual who insisted that his only reason for wanting to join the army was that he 'loved the uniform'!

The President of the Board, a surprisingly small Brigadier, opened the second day with some useful guidelines on how we should behave during the tests. This ranged from how he expected the groups of eight to operate in our use of the Mess during the evenings: "much as I admire individuality", he remarked, "and contrary to public opinion, I am not partial to the sound of bagpipes outside my bedroom window at six o'clock in the morning!" Indeed, the President did not appear to be partial to any previously conducted entertainments (written off as 'high spirits'), though he had us in hysterics throughout his speech. Concluding with a hint of sobriety he added: "And if you think that letting of the fire-extinguishers in the Mess is going to impress me, think again."

My group's opening discussion lasted for more than the scheduled forty minutes as we debated issues ranging from 'blood sports' to the 'Middle East Crisis'. All eight of us seemed knowledgeable in the subjects thrown at us and we threw our views across the room energetically, ensuring that each of us had a say in every topic. At least one of us would take up a contrary position in the ensuing debate, regardless of our personal beliefs, though as the talks continued, we settled into the views which we ultimately upheld in conversation later.

"What do you think of the present situation in Lebanon?" the invigilating Colonel asked.

"It appears to me that the solution to the conflict can only be attained through dialogue and that the Israelis and the Palestinians must get together and talk," stated George, in his upholstered Queen's English.

"I agree,"added Pete, a well built, chirpy Borderer destined for the Coldstream Guards, "the sooner the representatives sit down and talk, the sooner a settlement can be reached."

"Ultimately I expect that Israel will relinquish some territory to the Palestinians, but the problem will be to establish an atmosphere of trust and mutual cooperation," said Hugh astutely, getting his oar in as he did on every occasion, "do you agree?".

"I doubt very much whether Israel will even consent to talk to Gaddafi," added Tom nervously.

"But Libya make pretty lousy intermediaries anyway, they seem more interested in head-hunting the terrorists for their own war-games!" butted in James, rescuing Tom from his name-slip with a laugh.

"What we need is for Arafat and Shamir to get round the table with a United Nations presence," pointed out James matter-of-factly. I agreed and added that the solution must be along the lines of India and Pakistan. The Colonel moved the topic on to 'the role of architects in the inner cities'.

Towards the end of the discussion conversation flew at great speed around the circle of chairs. We all had a say and pitched into each topic with energy and fortitude. Ultimately the group closed ranks, welded together in a unity of purpose. This was to hold us in good stead in the outdoor tasks after lunch.

The 'Group Leader' briefed us on what the aim of each task was as we stood in front of the apparatus, dressed in khaki overalls and coloured bibs. The tasks were to be leaderless. After giving us our task, the Major stood back and listened as we each put forward our solution to the problem. Sometimes the solution would come straight away as one of us would hit upon a practical way to move the team from A to B; on other occasions one of us would put forward his idea and someone else would think of an easier method. As in the interviews we all ensured that we had our idea listened to and that the other members were in agreement. After the discussion and, having formulated and agreed upon our plan, the Group Leader asked one of us to give his version of how the obstacle should be crossed. Our minds were all in top gear, more concentrated than ever before so there was no question of any of us not having heard or understood the group solution. The Group Leader seemed to sense this and kept this part of the task short, letting us get on and accomplish each task as soon as possible.

The individual who was nominated to tell the Major how we proposed to complete the task was also asked how long he envisaged it would take us — usually twelve minutes. The Major surprised us by allowing us exactly the amount of time we had asked for. Once or twice we failed to complete the task in the allotted time, but we were kept at it until the obstacle in question had been crossed.

The tasks themselves involved carrying a heavy burden over or through a wooden construction without touching the ground between the start and the finish. This required a coordinated physical effort and sense of urgency. We achieved the former naturally: the bigger members of the team, of which

I was one, lifted and carried the burden, the smaller members tied knots and cleared the way. We kept track of time by appointing a time-keeper and took turns to spur each other on, more by accident than intention, though each of us wanted to be seen to be leading. In this way we maintained both the impetus and pace.

The team race that followed was a simple counter-lever operation involving a plank and rope, with ourselves as weights. It was a leaderless task and as the whistle blew all the competing teams shouted out their solutions. Placing the plank on my shoulder I knelt down on the bank of the ditch, with the long end of the plank reaching about two feet away from the other side.

"Hold the short end down, George!" I shouted, "Mike, run along the plank and jump the last few feet!" Mike sprung up and jumped nimbly over while George and I braced ourselves. The rest of the team followed suit and copied the method to bring George and me across. George was almost too heavy and it took what seemed an eternity to swivel him round on to the far bank, with everyone puffing and panting. We won the race and jogged happily back to the rooms for a shower.

A dozen of us waited in a sitting room, dressed in suits, to be called to our first interview. We could not hide the feeling of tense anticipation; conversation was muted and I glanced through books and newspapers, taking nothing in. What seemed an eternity was in fact less than ten minutes. I was called through to the Education Adviser, a Colonel in the Royal Army Education Corps, and was directed to sit down. I saw the large file in front of the Colonel and wondered how much the Army actually knew about me. The Colonel was initially interested in my motives for wanting to be an Officer, based on my background, but later geared the questions towards my education. I was asked whether I thought my academic results were good enough and whether I had considered going to university. They were and I had, but I put forward my intention to do an 'In-service degree' sponsored by the Army. This seemed to lighten the tone of the interview and we discussed my future career progression. I left the interview feeling that the world was my oyster!

The other two interviews, conducted by one of the three Vice-Presidents, a Colonel, and the Deputy President, a lieutenant Colonel, divided my life between my accomplishments, and my interests and ambitions and were almost entirely based upon what I had written on my application form.

"What do you consider to be the important attributes of an Officer?" asked the Vice-President in his interview. I rattled off some leadership qualities reminiscent of Montgomery:

"To be able to communicate instructions to your men and lead them to a common purpose; intelligence, by which I mean sound judgement and quick thinking; integrity; courage and, perhaps most importantly, humour

13

in the face of adversity," I replied.

"What about moral courage?" the Colonel asked, testingly.

"That I include in 'integrity', and is particularly important when an Officer is asked to make decisions between what is right and wrong," I replied.

"Do you believe you have these qualities?"

"Yes." The Colonel remained impassively silent so I continued: "based upon my experiences in Cadet training and on the Scottish 'O' type course, I believe I have the necessary temperament and qualifications."

"Good," commented the Colonel. "I would be surprised to see you here if you didn't think so," he added, smiling. I felt a glow of relief; "I'm on to a winner" I thought.

The Deputy President's interview was equally grilling, as my mind rapidly considered each question and what I considered the 'correct answer', in line with my interests and ambitions. Of course there were not any 'right answers' as such, but there were most certainly wrong answers, which could bring any potential Officer's career to an untimely end. I paused before each reply, focussing my mind on the real purpose of the question; "ambitious?" I thought, "should I say I want his job?"

"I intend to have a long and rewarding career in the Army, but I don't expect to accomplish a high rank overnight," I answered. "I think the best job to have is that of a Major, with the best combination of direct contact with the men and a good output of paperwork decisions, but I would like to command my chosen Regiment," I answered confidently.

"How long do you expect that to take?" the Deputy President demanded.

"Two years as a second lieutenant after Sandhurst, another two or three as a full lieutenant; five years as Captain, another five to seven as Major... I expect to make Colonel by the time I'm forty," I retorted.

"Good luck!" chuckled the Deputy and motioned to the door.

That night I telephoned Alice Liddell-Grainger, a close friend, to organise a weekend of London entertainment and rang my sister to accept the living room couch. 'An opportunity missed is one gone forever' I thought and I had decided not to waste the chance of 'living it up' in London.

The first half of Wednesday morning was taken up with a Planning Project. The problem I was given was one of an American Practice Nuclear Warhead going off-course and landing on an island in the Caribbean. I was some twelve miles away with my army adventurous training team, on board a steamer, when the Captain informed me that a radio message had been received from the Admiralty instructing me to find and protect the warhead as a Soviet submarine had been spotted in the area and the American Army could not reach the island for twelve hours. Further details of the problem were about the equipment and weapons on board and the geography of the island. There were apparently three landing areas: one, the nearest to us, involving a slow climb up a rockface; the second on a sandy beach further away and the third on the other side of the island. I chose the sandy beach and had a theoretical solution written out which ensured that my team would arrive several hours before the Russians could possibly be there. This involved some elementary mathematics: speed, distance and time equations, and the effective use of the section of men and the equipment available.

The time given for our individual, written solutions drew to a close just as I finished 'raising the Union Jack to the approaching Americans', but before I had offered them tea! For the next half hour my group discussed its solutions. I outlined my plan, but soon discovered that my next-door colleague had reached his warhead forty minutes earlier by climbing the rockface, which I had written off as 'being too dangerous to do overnight'. This became the group solution and we incorporated ideas from each member of the team. We discussed practicalities that might lead to other solutions and Hugh was invited to give the group solution to the problem to the Major.

The morning's activity continued unabated as we jogged out to the designated 'glorious turf' for further analysis. The Command Tasks we were faced with involved ropes, planks of wood and oil drums; indeed, a whole array of equipment. I was the first to be put in command, having the lowest number on my bib. We were all told to address each other by number, which although impersonal was useful to both the Major, our 'Group Leader', and to each of us as we took our turn in command. I was taken aside for a briefing and told to get the team from one side of the 'shark-infested waters' to the other using any equipment we needed, but taking across any equipment we used. In front of me was a horizontal pole, eight-feet high, stretching across the centre of the 'waters', held up by a tripod of poles on either side. These poles were not to be touched, I was told. On the ground in front lay two heavy oil drums, two poles and a coil of rope. I was given twelve minutes to complete my task.

Quickly gathering the group around me, I explained my plan and detailed tasks to each individual, not forgetting the ultimate military query "any questions?" George, who was the tallest of the group picked up the pole and hoisted it up to the crossbar, as it was too short to reach from ground level. Pete, Hugh, Tom and I then scrambled up over George onto the pole and up onto the crossbar. Mike took the pole from George as he was the lightest member of the group, and George swung up the pole to the crossbar, shouting "five minutes!" at the top of his voice...We managed to tow Mike up using the pole as a lever and swung him over to the other side of our imaginary river. The rest of us then slid down the pole beyond the chalk line denoting 'safety'.

The other Command tasks went equally smoothly and we were all feeling

"Brave effort number fifteen, any more bright ideas?"

16

quite confident by the end, chattering away merrily, when the Major approached us and said: "time for one more — number nine, you're on." We followed the Major to an area of ground littered with twenty or so small wooden stakes. A red tape denoted the start line and a blue one the finish. I was to cross the minefield with my team and two ammunition boxes (filled with bricks), without touching the ground, which the Major described as 'a minefield full of unmentionable torments' and without any of us touching the stakes. We were able to use six small planks of different lengths and a long heavy rope, which was not allowed to touch the ground either.

The solution seemed simple: we would simply place the planks on the stakes and bridge ourselves across. We were about half way through the task when the Major interrupted: "Stop there! That middle stake is out of bounds now." This left Pete on the far side; George on one plank holding an ammunition box; myself on another plank and Hugh out of the Task. The others were all on the starting side. We moved the planks and made another bridge enabling George to get across.

"That plank's out of bounds" shouted the Major pointing to the plank nearest the finish line. Time was running short. We re-routed the remaining four planks.

"The plank on the right is out of bounds!" instructed the Major as I sprung to safety. Tom and Mike now began to shuttle across using three planks. We had ten seconds left to go.

"Jump!" I shouted. Tom jumped clean onto our side of the blue tape; Mike landed just short.

"Dead!" shouted the Major, scribbling furiously on his pad of paper. I felt apprehensive, but the Major gave no clues: "team race!" he instructed, and we followed the direction of his gaze to the six-foot ditch.

Individually we were called over to attempt an array of obstacles scattered around the assault course area. Most of the obstacles had to be passed under, over or through carrying heavy ammunition boxes. The Group Leader took me round each obstacle indicating what had to be achieved, without saying how to achieve it: at a tree obstacle I was told that I had to reach a platform ten feet up and place a heavy ammunition box on it without touching the tree. I could only use the short rope that dangled at about head height. When I approached this obstacle on my way round I tried again and again to climb the rope with the ammunition box strapped on. After my third attempt I was about to give up, but the Major informed me that "having started an obstacle one had to see it through". I tied the box onto the rope and using a neat athletics trick I had learnt at school, hoisted my legs up vertically to the platform. With my feet now on the platform I pulled the rest of my body up and raised the rope and ammunition box. My time was up, but glancing at the Major I was sure he seemed pleased with my effort.

During the afternoon my group gathered in a small classroom for the scheduled 'Lecturettes'. We were each given a small selection of our own interests from which to choose a subject and about half an hour to prepare. At the end of each talk we discussed the subject matter with the speaker, usually phrasing our questions so that he could answer them in such a way as to increase his own 'image': Pete talked about sailing in the Mediterranean, so he was asked whether he had to overcome language barriers and tidal difficulties; Tom talked about his 'year off in Australia', and was asked about the difficulties of herding sheep on horseback. The questions were not planned, but we were all aware of the need to help each other along. I gave my talk on the 'Duke of Edinburgh's Award Scheme', which had taken up much of my free-time at school, making extensive use of the available blackboards.

That night I went to bed early, conscious of the hard day ahead. While I was asleep two or three individuals in the intake decided that their own brand of humour should be expressed and set to with a vengeance, throwing stolen thunderflashes into the bar area of the Mess. Over breakfast on Thursday we discovered to our surprise that they were being allowed to finish the Board and that the Brigadier had said "their action would not affect their individual results." It was later discovered that the three had already failed!

We had decided to add spice to the Final Race, on Thursday morning, by challenging the girls. The assault course in front of us contained a mixture of rope, frame and plank obstacles painted green, with 'out of bounds' areas painted red. We volunteered Mike, as the lightest of us, to act as the 'body', while we built a rudimentary stretcher around him. I volunteered to lead off, being quick on the ropes, followed by George, who was to pull everyone up. (The girls had the advantage of a ladder up the rope obstacles). The starting pistol fired - we were off! I hoisted myself up the rope ladder and started pulling the others up. "Go on! Go on!" George shouted. I raced on over the frame and across the swing ropes to the third obstacle. There were two bars in front of us, waist high, separated by a space of six feet — 'too far to jump' I thought aloud. The rule for this obstacle was that only one of the group was allowed to go under the bars. An idea flashed into my mind. I scrambled under the first bar and braced myself on all fours in the middle ground.

"Step on my shoulders and jump across!" I ordered. Sensing some hesitation I repeated myself, adding "Move it!" as an added incentive. I felt the team step rapidly across my back, lighter than I had expected. The stretcher held us up for a brief moment and I felt George step nimbly across with a loud "Last man" to me. I scrambled under the second bar and leaped across the seven remaining obstacles, sensing the encouragement of the team as they gathered over the finish line. We freed Mike from his uncomfortable bed and formed up in ranks, noticing the girls on our flank do likewise. "A draw!" we cried emphatically to the feminine shrieks of "We won!". We had in fact beaten the other teams by several seconds and moved across to clap-in the last group.

The President of the Board summed up the few days as he'd seen them, talked about the pass rate and how some of us "would be given the opportunity to build upon our leadership qualities in Rowallen Company", a pre-Sandhurst course infamous for its 'toughening-up' barbarity and as alien to 'an exciting job' as pressing the button on an office photocopier. I prayed for a 'straight pass'.

After a weekend of restaurants and nightclubs I returned to the Scottish Infantry Depot, Glencorse Barracks, near Edinburgh, to return my 'O' type uniform. After receiving my final pay slip I was ushered in to see the Colonel.

"Congratulations Salvesen" he said, as I stood bolt upright before him, "Out of the twelve potential Officers on your course, you and Laidlaw have won places at Sandhurst. Laidlaw got Rowallen and you may as well know that I recommended you for that too, so well done: I hope you realise how much the course has done for you."

"Yes Sir. Thank you" I said, deciding it would be wrong to add anything further. At least I had proved myself. I returned home for a family celebration.

CHAPTER TWO : FIRST ENCOUNTER

My first impressions of the Royal Military Academy were of the magnificent architecture of Old College, standing in grandeur within the seven hundred acres or so of playing fields, woods and lakes. It seemed timeless and unshakable: a statement of pride of a proud nation. Statues appeared in one or two places adding a further touch of glory and the entire surroundings were spotlessly clean. New College, where I was to spend the next twelve months of sheer survival, was a less impressive building architecturally, being of Victorian brick and mortar. It was to be my home for the next year, housing many of the classrooms and most of the sleeping accommodation. Victory College, the ugliest of the Sandhurst Colleges, housed the graduate students and was separated from New College by the Wishstream, a burn which connected the two lakes and doubled as an obstacle in the assault course: a feat described as a 'concurrent activity' at Sandhurst and one which was heartily encouraged. Up in the Redoubt, an area to the north of the main buildings, Rhine and Salerno Companies bustled around the ageing 'temporary accommodation'; wooden buildings where preservation was the order of the day. The extra distance to the classrooms offered few comforts and the Redoubt was nick-named 'Coventry' on account of its isolation.

I was the last of my platoon to arrive, having been collected by a worn out Colour Sergeant in a green army minibus at Camberley Station, along with the eight other Potential Officers who had delayed their purgatory to the last moment; I was not expecting to enjoy my time at Sandhurst, taking the attitude that it was a course to be endured, like a course of foul tasting medicine. Directed into a large ante-room beside the guard room of New College, I joined the queue of emblazered civilians, to be issued with my platoon, my company, my army number "to be memorised", my plastic name tag "to be worn at all times" and a rapid succession of directions in colloquial military jargon.

My Platoon Colour Sergeant found me before I had found him and greeted me with the sound proclamation "I knew you'd be the last, Mr.

Salvesen... You and I are going to get along just fine." I already hated the place. Half an hour later we were paraded outside our company 'lines' for initial inspection. Colour Sergeant Thomson wandered along the line issuing instructions for the next day, at the same time pointing out offending items of civilian dress which were "not to be seen again". I had bought a pair of smart suede shoes that day and stood proudly in the knowledge that no possible fault could be discovered. Alas, my purchase became my penalty..."I never want to see these again, you may as well throw them away"... I hid the offending items in my suitcase in eager anticipation of a 'pip' on the shoulder and an easier lifestyle.

Inside the Alamein Lines we were herded into our platoon classroom, adjacent to the New College Bar, to meet 'the Team'.

Colour Sergeant Thomson introduced us to our Platoon Commander, Captain Sexton, whom we soon discovered was an Oxbridge high-flyer distinguished by a handful of Blues and degrees. With a methodology particular to the Royal Engineers, we were talked through Captain Sexton's expectations, leaving me in little doubt as to the high standard I would have to achieve. The class was handed over to our platoon Sergeant and with an expressionless face he talked us through 'behaviour in the lines', adding that "the bar will be shut until you pass off the Square at the end of the fifth week for those of you who make it". I felt hearts sink all around me. In contrast to the casual first evening of acclimatization and introductions, the whirl of new kit dispensing and introductory talks swamped the next day and from then on I was not to manage more than three hours of sleep per night for the next five weeks. Everyone in my platoon anticipated the harsh treatment for which Sandhurst is renowned. Sure enough, it arrived: homing in on us like a cruise missile. Dressed in an assortment of suits, tweed jackets and blazers we were marched rapidly, and in a flurry of skipped paces, to the Academy Quartermaster's stores one and a half miles away, to be issued with "trousers, lightweight, two; boots, drill; laces two, boots for the use of... and several bags full of other items to be transported manually back to our lines. The measuring of boots, Sandhurst Blues and number two dress took over an hour as we stumbled around collecting all the necessary accessories along the 'conveyor belt' system, so Colour Sergeant Thomson left us to our own devices and we staggered back to our rooms laden with clothes of all descriptions in dribs and drabs.

The other 'Gentlemen' were as keen to learn about me as I was about them, starting, as we then thought, from a base of equality. However, it soon became apparent that the former soldiers, members of Rowallan Company (the character-building pre-Sandhurst Course) and of Brigade Squad (the Guards potential officers' course) were far beyond my standard of training, which perhaps gave an unfair advantage. Those of Rowallan Company had already received months of gruelling drill, physical exertion and intimidation; for them the army could do no worse.

The shelter of my personal room came complete with desk, bed and wardrobe, 'shoebox' safe and 'lounge lizard' armchair, I pinned my nametag to the bright red tracksuit, draping the sports jacket and tie of the first few days on my bed, left the 'home comforts' and joined the platoon for our march to the session of 'identikit' appointments. Pay interviews were followed by identity photography and rounded off with our first paperchase. The foreign students joined us for the day, having received separate 'V.I.P.' introductions.

At this embryonic stage in our military development, some interesting pointers had already been established. The Churchill Hall, our main lecture theatre, was warmly referred to as 'the slumberhall' and we were told that "if you fall asleep there, it will be 'un-cool'"! This was made dramatically clear in our first introductory talk by the Commandant, when venomous instructors took to the steps of the lecture room to prod offending dreamers with their pace-sticks.

Dressed impeccably in the uniform of the Scots Guards, and every now and then brushing his moustache with the thumb of his right hand, Colour Sergeant Thomson prided himself on his perfect turnout, his years of experience and his unblemished record. He had risen rapidly through the ranks of his chosen regiment, finding his natural flair for imparting knowledge a great asset. We were his second Platoon at Sandhurst, but Colour Sergeant Thomson's energy was boundless. Learning the basic steps of drill became an art, to be accompanied by goading roars of "You're a Lunatic, Sir!" We addressed Colour Sergeant Thomson as 'Staff' as we did all the Non-Commissioned Officers. They took as much pride in this as we did in being called 'Sir', but *we* were severely reprimanded if we called *them* 'Sir' — they had no intention of being Officers, we were informed. Every question asked of us was to be replied in unison with the answer 'Staff' and there was no alternative. And thus we were instructed, with insults and fierce encouragement, littered with epithets that made drill bearable: "About turn to the right, you horrible excuse of a soldier! If you swivel to the left once more I'll volunteer you for duty at the Bleedin' Kremlin, Sir! I didn't get where I am today idly reminiscing!" Thus 'square-bashing' became a game of wit and prescription and that bit more endurable.

Our first visit to Mr. Jones was one of the less pleasurable initiatives of the first week. At a pound a time, Mr. Jones wasn't going to waste precious taxpayer's money creating the finery of a Saville Row cut. So loved were his thirty-second, cosmetic sheep-shaves that the last course through Sandhurst had bricked-up the barber's shop entrance! An escape to the gymnasium, however, was a contradiction in terms. The Physical Training Instructors were of the unanimous opinion that we were unfit to be in the

"A week of PT and it'll fit you like a glove, Sir"

"This is not Barbados, Sir. You will not need the quick-tan coconut oil here!"

British Army, and set to with a vengeance to sort us out. Circuit training was prescribed, and those who turned up without spotlessly clean uniforms, starched to perfection, received personal attention. We were made aware that our physical performance was being closely monitored and would be included in our grading every month. I made a mental note to whitewash my gymshoes that evening.

It became clear to me, as the weekend approached, that The Grand Old Duke of York was not, in fact, dreaming when he marched his ten thousand men up and down the hill (as the nursery rhyme has it) — he was really teaching them to 'Pace!'. The platoon did quite a considerable amount of marching and pacing during the first few days; a painful, but invigorating process which reaped its rewards in the night exercises. The idea was to count, at every speed, how many paces it takes to cover a hundred metres. In this way distances were measured in dense fog and at night when landmarks could be seen. This exercise was carried out on a particularly grim night march when Crispin Bond, an experienced ex-squaddie, led us through marsh and fog to spring the proverbial dawn attack.

Tennis was yet another opportunity to flex my muscles, though only at Company level. When taken by our Colour Sergeant, whose bark was only surpassed by his bite, playing tennis was great fun. His aptitude for winning was infectious. We soon had a fervent desire built in us to win. Indeed, so enthusiastic was he that he jumped for joy every time he won a point — and sometimes even when he lost one! Seeded fifth in the Company I often had the opportunity of proving my worth. I played Colour Sergeant Thomson several times in Tennis Doubles, away from the drill-square, where discipline was temporarily relaxed. So while he was entertaining us with a metaphoric lap of honour, it was quite permissible to state, in a loud, clear voice: "but it was *out* Staff!"

This in itself had marvellous side-effects: the platoon quickly pooled its resources and, strengthened with an inner spirit of absolute determination, shone with the brilliance of unity, in the knowledge that "he's human after all".

That kind of situation comedy was confined to the tennis courts. Off court there was no opportunity for 'off the cuff' remarks — only for hard work. And the more effort I put into it, the more I enjoyed it. It was with a great deal of difficulty, however, that I managed to iron kit and make copious notes during the first week, as some comedian had equipped my table lamp with a dark blue bulb!

We were lucky to have a very understanding padre, and church on Sunday became our only refuge from sleepless torture. In the chapel we were told that "it's perfectly alright if you sleep through the Services — just as long as you let me (The Reverend P. T. Clement C. F.) sleep too"!

One of the most fun activities of the week occurred on the Sunday, when we had to construct lecturettes about ourselves and present the finished product in a five-minute talk to the rest of the platoon. One comic example was of an anonymous Officer-Cadet's recital of 'Ski-bumming' in France. "This", we were told, "is a kind of holiday only to be undertaken by the very macho and *only* at the risk of losing one's moral fibre! It entails financing one's skiing by begging off Chalet Girls, of whom there is an abundance." Apparently, on this particular trip there were about "two hundred Chalet Girls with only fifty Bums"!

Another Officer Cadet gave his account of a job, working in an ice-cream cold store. One of the most memorable activities was playing a form of indoor cricket, using a frozen, seventeen pound salmon as a bat; a frozen potato as the ball and scoring by hitting the different flavours of ice-cream! One particular day, one of the workmen scored a six, hitting the 'Rum and Raisin' variety and let out a squeal of delight. Simultaneously, the manager opened the door...The game has since been called 'It's a Knockout'!

These moments of self-expression showed that despite the hard training and fatigue, the team-spirit of my platoon, with its humour in the face of adversity, made the workload bearable. We had arrived at Sandhurst from a variety of backgrounds: State school, Public school, foreign armies and from the ranks of the regular British army. As a consequence there were differences in ages, from eighteen to twenty-four, and accent, from Iraqui to Welsh and from Queen's English to broad Yorkshire. Some of us had Army backgrounds, others were completely new to it all. For sheer preservation we had to 'muck-in' together, sharing the tasks of cleaning and polishing the corridors into the early hours; helping each other build 'bed-blocks' and regularise our rooms. I was in the room next to Tony Moore, who had been a Corporal in the Royal Engineers. Together we managed to make it through the painful first few weeks by learning the system and implementing a routine. Many mistakes were made and it was an uphill struggle learning from my mistakes and building on them. Tony kept me on the right track and I ploughed on with as much fortitude as I could muster. Throughout the course the Officer Cadets who had come from the ranks helped the rest of us along. Mick Gallagher was an invaluable support. He was a quiet, unassuming man whom we nick-named 'Grandad': he had been an instructor in the skill-at-arms wing of Sandhurst only a few weeks before and had chosen to experience the course for himself rather than wait for the automatic Commission that would have eventually come his way. With Mick's guidance we anticipated the events before us and prepared for them in advance.

As the volume of 'tactical verbals' increased on the drill square, so did the platoon's coordination, though still far from perfect. The Colour Sergeant expressed a remarkable breadth of vocabulary and an incomparable way with words:

"Hit for six"

27

"I'll have you spitting out raw meat and nails by the end of the Fifth week, Cedric!"...Of course there were a few derogatory expressions too — but protocol forbids...Our platoon Commander too, had the knack of extracting mirth: our exhausting five mile run into the Barossa woods was described as "a little therapeutic exercise"! Unlike the Non-Commissioned Officer Drill instructors, who were picked almost exclusively from the Brigade of Guards, the Officers were hand-picked from all the British regiments and corps and were consequently the 'high flyers' of the Army: the future Colonels, Brigadiers and Generals.

Back in the lines, my evenings were spent shining my boots — so energetically, in fact, that the polish rubbed off, on and off again, in a rhythmic cycle of frustration. 'Calves may come, grow-up and leave, but the Bull in this place goes on for ever!' Having created a basic glow on the boots, I was further frustrated into cracking it all on the Drill Square. I was, however, particularly good at shining brass buckles, and could brush polish ordinary boots with ease. So when we gathered for a supervised session of *bulling*, I swapped my drill boots for one of the others' buckles. I found myself constantly being reminded of the words of Monty Python: "But it's ALL for the good of the Country!"(?)

CHAPTER THREE: FIVE WEEKS OF SATIRE

The first five weeks of Sandhurst life had to be borne with clenched fists and ground teeth. Routinely there was 'drill' to both enjoy and endure, initially in red tracksuits: one Officer Cadet commented "I feel like a Bloody Mary, Staff"; the Colour Sergeant's reply shot back: "You look like one too, Miss...er, Sir!" Thereafter we paraded in khaki green Barrack dress. We survived a tight timetable of weapon training, physical training and lectures which required changing uniform every forty minutes. This instilled an atmosphere of continuous pressure and a determination to see the day through. False confidence gave way to team spirit; slow methodology to hyper-activity. Our 'Texaco Forecourt' appearance transformed into soldierly uniformity.

Reveille was at six o'clock. By six fifteen the corridor was full of enquiries as to what dress we were to wear and whether anyone else knew!

Kicking off with a muster parade straight after breakfast we often felt the wield of Sergeant power even before we were fully awake. We were properly kitted-out in khaki and our boots glinted in the early morning sun. On the few occasions that they did not glint, there was no reprieve. 'Restrictions of Privilege', shortened to R.O.P.s or 'ropes' were handed out with a generosity not even encountered at Christmas! This entailed parading after every meal and in perfect order in front of the Duty N.C.O., invariably someone else's Colour Sergeant.

"Defaulters, Defaauullterrs....SHUN!"

A loud, authoritative voice shattered my contemplations. I braced-up instinctively and carried out the drill movement without thinking, staring at the picture of the Battle of Alamein on the wall five feet in front of me.

Addressed as 'defaulters', we were to stand to attention for what seemed like an eternity, while the Duty N.C.O. moved along the line. It was a vicious circle: parade, error, parade... mistakes in turnout were plucked out from thin air; a drifting piece of dust would be spotted gliding downwards, and the whole line prayed it would land on someone else, who would be generously awarded three further R.O.P.s. The restrictions also kept us from

29

"Are you marching to the same battle Mr Smith?"

Platoon duties and the evening visits to Macdonald's to supplement our diets.

Every now and then the Company Sergeant Major would march out of his office to inspect us, which led, as often as not, to the entire Platoon being paraded again that night. Sergeant Major Lynch suited his name. He was not a man to be meddled with. My first inspection by this fearsome Irish Guardsman stuck in my mind for weeks. We had all been marched forward and formed in 'Open Order' to be inspected. Colour Sergeant Lynch had this movement alone repeated three times until he was satisfied. Half the first row were exchanged with the third row as they "didn't look handsome enough", and then changed back again when it was pronounced that we were "all a bunch of ugly bastards, unfit to serve in an asylum let alone the British army!" When he reached me I was preparing to be marched away to the Guardroom.

"What is this miserable excuse for a civilian doing in your Platoon, Colour Sergeant?" he asked, glaring at me, "has he any conceivable talents?" Without a moment's hesitation Colour Sergeant Thomson replied, raising a line of smiles along the rank, "He can play the piano, Sir." I was caught by surprise, it must have been on my record of interests.

"Oh, well that's alright then," said Sergeant Major Lynch, walking on to the next sinner, "Let's hear a few tunes sometime." It was only later that I discovered that Sergeant Major Lynch was a keen singer, endowed with one of the best voices to be heard at Sandhurst.

Only eight of us escaped the much expected restrictions that night, the others were all to become Platoon Corporals and Under Officers.

Every few days we would parade outside our rooms rather than on the square, dressed for the first lesson. Colour Sergeant Thomson inspected the rooms carefully, encouraging us to look at each others' rooms so that everything would be uniform, and warning against 'dust'. The evenings were invariably spent tidying rooms, and even polishing the stairs with shoe-polish and Brasso! In our rooms at night there was not much room for sleep as there were Room Inspections daily and all the items of uniform (and civilian clothes) had to be presented in a soldierly manner. This in effect meant that all compressable items were reduced to A4 (and it's amazing what could be compressed!) and other items that must show immaculate creases were hung in a pre-designated order. The necessity of showing neatly turned-out bedblocks every morning meant that most of us slept in sleeping bags, leaving the sheets wrapped in blankets for the Adjutant to inspect in the morning. Although no-one threw litter outside there was a permanent supply to be collected every morning: the sight of a wasted piece of paper gave the Colour Sergeant a hernia! The 'Emu-bobbing' sessions also provided time to look for bombs, just in case anyone thought that Military Security was a contradiction in terms;

31

apparently that only applied to the Intelligence Corps!

Each lesson required a different form of dress, and to give us plenty of variety the lessons were arranged in such a way that we started with drill, moved on to weapon training and then to signals training. During these first five weeks, and indeed on to the tenth week, we never stopped running, marching, drilling, saluting and polishing until we were blue in the face. Even shooting was energy consuming as we ran backwards and forwards to the ranges; on to the butts; pasted the targets and ran back again, only pausing when someone had a negligent discharge (N.D.). In the gymnasium, gymshoes and belts had to be scrubbed before they were whitened, so that no hint of dirt showed through, but if several coats were put on and the paint cracked, "there were many more punishments that could be utilised". On most days we were given fifteen minutes between being dismissed from one lesson and being paraded for the next, in which time we had to run as a platoon back to our lines, change, re-assemble and 'double' to the next location. The least punishment for being late was an earful of abuse, the most was explaining yourself to the Platoon Commander. My first parade before the Platoon Commander was an awesome experience. I was dressed in my Sandhurst Blues, inspected by a disenchanted Colour Sergeant Thomson and marched in to Captain Sexton's room, a distance of six feet, at the double. Ground to a halt I shouted out my name, rank and number and awaited his judgement. The severity of the punishment was much less than the act of being charged itself, but it was an experience we were all put through. I was awarded 'two days Restriction of Privilege'.

Mealtimes were the highlight of the day and were characterised by the Colour Sergeant's description of them as 'mid-flight re-fuelling'. The frantic activity of rushing from one lecture to another in double-quick time meant that I consumed vast platefuls of food, but so as not to waste any precious telephoning time, this was done in double-quick time too! Being a connoisseur of 'Cordon Bleu' (and even Cordon Negro), I took particular care to diagnose the viscosity of the processed peas, the vintage of the orange squash and the pliability of the steaks! Finding this process remarkably beneficial I applied for the post of Messing Member, to which I was duly appointed. This resulted in the provision of extra rations, warm toast and occasionally a biscuit at tea-time! In fact the committee had little influence over the day to day running of the kitchens as it was felt that the consumers would be biassed!

We had all been issued with plastic name tags and these stayed on until the Directing Staff had learnt all our names. As we changed uniform no less than four times a day the pins warped and broke leaving the task of enduring the Company Sergeant Major's wrath when we asked for a re-issue. It was quite a task for us to learn each other's names: within the platoon this came

32

rapidly — a matter of survival — but outside the company there were just so many strangers. We had the Staff names to register too and to this end we were given a sheet of all the academy staff we would come across, to be committed to memory: we would be tested! Of course there were one or two individuals we hated the sight of , if only because of the reaction that was predicted. The 'Enemy' were defined as 'an overt force identifiable by crowns and pips on epaulettes or crowns and stripes on sleeves'. Occasionally we had advance warning from the distant clicketty-clop of an approaching horse: direct contact with the Adjutant was to be avoided at all costs as he would undoubtedly pick you up for some misdemeanour! But the worst thing was to mistake a graduate student for an Officer of the Directing Staff: saluting graduates showed a lack of street credibility!

Mr. Jones was also to be avoided if at all possible. Living as he did in a barber's shop in New College, Mr. Jones averaged, by his own reckoning fifty haircuts a day of the *very* short back and sides variety. We reported to have a haircut every two weeks at this stage in the course and thereafter once a month at the discretion of the staff. Hair was not allowed to be shorn to American standards either, it had to be tapered to just the right length: no more, no less. Moustaches had to be watched too, though few Officer Cadets had one: "above the lip it's all yours, below the lip and it belongs to the Adjutant!"

Some elementary Principles of Warfare were taught by our Platoon Commander in the classroom lessons during the first five weeks, of which 'flexibility' and 'simplicity' became key words of tactical importance. 'Economy of Effort' had already registered in our survival techniques, as much as keeping a low profile had become important in avoiding any 'harassing fire'. Military jargon was impressed upon us from all angles: from the deadly vu-foils of the classroom to the exercises amongst the ferocious gorse bushes of the Barossa. On many of these occasions Captain Sexton, our Platoon Commander would accompany us. He was well versed in infantry tactics, though he was a Royal Engineer at heart, and an extremely well read man. Always keeping a distance between himself and us — "familiarity breeds contempt" — his blend of educated humour and common sense made a marked impression upon the Platoon. He took an interest in our social lives as well as our military performance, and taught most of our classroom lessons, from the basics of map-reading, to the intricacies of social etiquette. Map-reading became all important, and Captain Sexton often led us out into the woods of the Barossa Valley, at the back of Sandhurst, to put the principles he had taught into practice. On one of these occasions we had our first introduction to camouflage: "cam cream is good for you", said Colour Sergeant Thomson "it builds up your zits and ensures that your wash your face every day!" — after applying the army issue mud to our faces many of us ended up looking more like characters

33

out of *Apocalypse Now* than Officer Cadets from deepest Surrey! Eventually a night navigation exercise was planned, and the undergrowth of the Barossa became as familiar to us by night as by day.

On one of my runs in the Barossa, returning via the assault course, I landed off the six foot wall on one ankle, snapping the tendons in a moment of excruciating pain. The run stopped instantly and I was carried up the road to the Military hospital. Y-listing is a medical form of back-terming, whereby students are put into classes in Old College until they are fit and then join the next intake to continue the Course. I was determined to stay with my platoon and rushed around from lesson to lesson on crutches: you can zip along the roads remarkably quickly on crutches! Once more the platoon pulled together and helped me along, carrying me upstairs and along to meals so as not to be late: even Colour Sergeant Thomson carried me upstairs! With physiotherapy every other day and a determination to get fit rapidly, I soon abandoned the crutches and retained only a walking stick until the end of the fifth week.

Two Officer Cadets from my platoon had already thrown in the towel, despising the training and conscious of less physical careers in 'civvy street'. The training staff kept the pressure on us, regularly humiliating an individual in front of the entire company or awarding 'extras' to the day's sinners. We were constantly compared with the senior division and rebuked as "unworthy so much as to serve them coffee", or words to that effect.

"I'm sure we're going to enjoy ourselves at Sandhurst aren't we?" pointed out Colour Sergeant Murray, another Scots Guard, "if you've got probs, you've got to catch me at the right moment. There'll be times you feel like crying. It's great!"

The regular supply of mail kept all our spirits up and our social life beyond the army was a feature of everyday conversation. Even the most heartfelt pains were swept away in the Lines. 'Dear John' letters were pinned to the notice board in jollity: "it is better to have loved and lost than never to have loved at all!" I pointed out to the cheering crowd. It was the tradition for the entire platoon to involve itself in personal affairs as much as in a platoon attack: the custom was that on receipt of a 'Dear John' every member of the platoon would write to the girl in question telling her how cruel she had been. Likewise, if a member of the platoon decided to give up an attractive partner, the platoon would write condolences and offer their individual attention! I was regularly asked in letters from friends what I *did* in the army, to which replies along the lines of "we iron our boots and shave our berets!" became popular.

The culmination of the Fifth week was the Drill Parade; 'Passing off the Square'. This is the point at which an Officer Cadet reaches the same standard of drill and turnout that a private soldier achieves after a less intensive 21 weeks. Consequently the build-up is tense and full of last

34

"The assault course"

minute re-adjustments. Colour Sergeant Thomson too was tense. Our success was a testament to his ability and it was customary for the Staff to lay bets on their students' performance — on how many of the platoon would pass. The rehearsal before the event was electric. Our Colour Sergeant made Dracula look like the Secretary General of the Red Cross! As he roared out commands the Platoon systematically moved around the Square, in unison and with stiff upper lips — totally expressionless faces united in concentration. Passing off the Square was achieved under the 'wet weather' auspices of Victory College, under the direction of the Adjutant. I was exempt the Parading as I still walked around with a stick, but managed to pass on the turnout, which gave me an overall pass. I watched as the rest of the Platoon hammered around the Square listening intently for someone to make a mistake... Ten minutes later our first major hurdle had been cleared.

That weekend was our first opportunity to escape from the sobriety of Sandhurst and make up for the weeks of frustration and indoctrination. No-one was allowed out for the weekend until they had passed off the Square. Luckily we all did. Almost without exception the course headed towards London, where the attraction of 'the Sandhurst man' to the girls we met at parties, if not the cropped haircut, was sure to be tested. This was the opportunity to test one's 'street credibility' and it was not to be missed... most of us, however, were so tired we spent our first weekend's leave catching up on lost sleep!

CHAPTER FOUR: HIGH SPIRITS

The arrival of the French Military school of St. Cyr was marked by some irony. At the time the newspapers were making a big thing out of the anniversary of the Battle of Waterloo: "For the Napoleonic Association this is very big bananas indeed"! (Sunday Times). Still, the French arrived and were split up into 'petit fours' attached to individual Officer Cadets. Primarily, the military nature of the visit had to be instilled, so we started the morning off teaching them how to march properly. As we marched around the Academy with our audience following in song behind, the Adjutant kept leap-frogging by; word went round that he enjoyed being saluted so much, he couldn't resist coming back for more! However, our Colour Sergeant was lapping it up, bursting out into fits of sporadic wit and letting fly "this is the meaning of life!" at every opportunity, in his broad Scots accent.

The singing went on and on....and on. Our French counterparts are taught how to sing as part of their training and seemed unable to move from A to B without a rendition of 'Frère Jacques' or some other bon mot. Consequently we made up a rebuffment jingle listing all the battles that we had beaten the French in, set to the tune of 'Frère Jacques'! The title of the song was duly scribbled in as 'Diplomacy' and was learnt by heart and sung to the French after Dinner. This 'pièce de resistance' was kept up long after the Loyal Toasts and Pate, in the Ante-Room where good hosting forced an epidemic of anaesthesia! The main topic of conversation revolved around the Adjutant and "how splendid he looked upon his horse". Fortified by the growing atmosphere of good will and boastful daring, this topic gave way to a comparison of the aerodynamics of the Adjutant to that of the Sergeant Major. This resulted in the poor men being given an early morning lesson in the art of flying from an encircled army blanket to the Mess ceiling and back! And rumour has it that both men quite enjoyed the experience!

We entertained our allies with several infantry skirmishes over the two weeks of their visit, continuing with our drill, physical training, skill at arms (weapon training) and the new instruction in administration and military organisation while the French were being entertained by the graduate students. After a week of watching exercises and general run-of-the-mill training, the French tour was grinding to a halt. The hierarchy decided to give them a good send-off with 'an education in British culture'. This kicked off in the early evening, after a quick supper, in the main halls of New College, where I helped host a cocktail party, being able to communicate, to a limited extent, in pidgin French. Outside, the transport was waiting to whisk us all off to London, ostensibly to show our guests the sights. While the majority of us remained indoors sipping glasses of Champagne or sherry, a team of covert warriors was turning the transport into Battle buses stacked with a choice collection of beer and plugged with quadraphonics. As the convoy left the Regulations of Sandhurst the Party began in earnest...

Socially, London could never be described as dead and on this occasion it was as alive as I have ever seen it. Leaving the buses near Piccadilly Circus, we descended on the city nightlife with a vengeance. So as not to crowd the clubs, we had previously picked out where each group was to go and so it was with trepidation that I set foot in the Café de Paris. My tour stretched through the night into many of the dimly-lit discos of London's West End, from the Hippodrome 'pick-up joint' in the East, to Crazy Larry's in the West and into many of the more upmarket clubs in between. The French had an uphill struggle in proving themselves more virile, and one can only presume the girls knew which side their bread was buttered! The French, of course, had much shorter haircuts than us — and ours were pretty short: theirs were skinhead and not pretty at all!

At this point in our Sandhurst lives, when a free evening could be discovered, the 'Slug and Lettuce' often figured in the quest to find a compatible partner. This was a wonderful pub, not far from Camberley, where the Winkfield Ladies congregated, sometimes to meet up with Officer Cadets and become part of the regimental groupees, sometimes for a drink. The former generally incorporates being invited to The Commissioning Ball and many Regimental functions in the aftermath. Some mothers go out of their way to ensure that their daughters go to the Commissioning Ball, which must be the best yuppie Ball in the country! A distinction should be made between 'Yuppies' and 'Sloanes', as these were seen at Sandhurst parties in abundance: Yuppies were taken by definition as Young Upwardly-mobile Professional People who had been at school or university with their Sandhurst counterparts; 'Sloanes' were generally the girls with all the finesse of a good family upbringing but without the brains. 'Blonde bombshells' fell into this category. The Winkfield Ladies and partying partners from various Eastbourne colleges fell somewhere in between. There were some who could use their brains but preferred to cook, and some without much intent to do either! For one of our more adventurous platoon parties, to generate some variety and spice, we had managed to

"Highland dancing"

39

"Company party"

persuade forty hairdressers from Poole to attend and these were definitely in the Sloane category!

By the eighth week of Sandhurst, parties were beginning to evolve and I took great pleasure in organising these tremendous occasions along with the other platoon eccentrics. Each party had its own individual theme and location: starting with "...When the ship went down...", in the pavilion, beside the boating lake; through to the platoon 'Silly Hat Party' in Camberley and digressing to the Women's Royal Army Corps toga party, with many Beagle Balls in between. Scottish Reels parties were always worth setting-off to, as well. They were held in Victory College and had a cult following of Scots, Scottish Officers (not necessarily the same thing), English and other nationalities and the regular assortment of 'good fun birds', thus becoming a favourite hunting ground. The reels themselves gave ample opportunity to size up the opposition, while the bar provided space for a less complicated approach, where witty performances of war stories were used to compete for the attention of the female guests. Those that succeeded in both aspects, so much so as to be noticed by the directing Colonel were unscrupulously paired-off and invited as a couple to the next Divisional Dinner party! Besides the Colonels' daughters, many of the female guests came from Winkfield, but occasionally individuals and groups were invited from as far afield as Reading. It was here that I met Dana Shaul, one of the most charismatic Winkfield girls — and created one of the many friendships that were to survive my military career. Dana, like many Winkfield Ladies, was constantly courted by Officer Cadets and kept the one or two she went out with strung around her little finger until their demise, though occasionally she was unaware of this. She was a natural dancer and picked up the intricacies of reeling with ease, while others floundered at the simplest 'Pas de Basque'. Whenever Captain Campbell, our Scottish Platoon Commander, found himself free of partners Crispin Swayne made sure either Dana or one of the other Winkfield Ladies asked him "for the next fling" while making a bee-line for Susan, Captain Campbell's stunningly attractive fiancé! Reeling was never to be taken too seriously and the cocktail of Victory College, New College, Officers and guests provided a welcome retreat from the 'Manual of Military Law', where the bravado, if not the derring-do of each individual was rewarded with a duty-free dram!

The pavilion parties were always tremendous fun. One particular Company party started more slowly than usual, the 'when the ship went down' party; guests and hosts drifted across the cricket pitch and others orienteered their way through the woods following the sound of the music, until the arrival of London's 'top discotheque' precipitated a mad dash for the dance floor. Colour Sergeant Thomson arrived in style, dressed in brightly coloured bermuda shorts and shirt, complete with matching cap, and wearing a blown up inflatable belt around his middle. For the first time, his wife came along too, and we could see the devotion that supported *him* through our exercises, late nights of bulling boots and long hours away from home. Bopping, jiving, twisting and ducking we managed to create such a flourish of synchronised colours that the Company Commander spotted us from one of the College windows. Under the mistaken belief that we were rehearsing for the forthcoming production of Slimmer's 'Sausage Machine (a mass requiem)', he strolled out to join us and has been boogying irregularly ever since! The cooks soon had a veritable banquet of comestibles smoking on the barbeque and the crowd split between the dance floor and the picnic tables. The party progressed with more and more beaming faces arriving, until the lakeside was quite crowded. Some Officer Cadets became so anaesthetised with the passing of events that a rendition of Rowan Atkinson was undertaken: "when two or three are gathered together, they shall perform the parrot sketch......."

"It is an ex-parrot."

"It has ceased to be..."

This unison of performing artists soon summoned up the courage to announce a boat race challenge in an off-the-cuff manner. The course was across the lake to an island and back and there were no rules. Consequently, as the flares lit up the sky and midnight struck, a mini-flotilla of crafts and canoes set off across the water at high speed, being constantly overturned and pirated en route. The Ladies joined into the spirit of the occasion, forming their own team, which unfortunately capsized! The oarsmen arrived back on shore drenched to the skin and dried off on the dance floor, slow dancing with their female guests, who were thoroughly soaked by this stage anyway. The mixture of sodden Officer Cadets, graduate students and partners with clinging wet clothes was a sight worth seeing! The steam evaporating off the more talented dancers shrouded the spectacle with a thin film of mystery....a mystery which would occupy rumour control for at least a week!

By three o'clock in the morning most of us had dried up and had the last quick drink and slow dance before the pickled bimble back across the turf to the accommodation. Coaches laden with Chiltern nursery nurses and Norlands' nannies sped past the guardroom towards the relative safety beyond.

CHAPTER FIVE: SOLDIERING ON

Rifle drill was a significant addition to the military curriculum and involved both coordination and effort. The movements required a thorough knowledge of the principles of Braille as the weapon must be moved into positions all around the body. This had to be achieved without so much as a furtive glance at the weapon. Furthermore one had to coordinate marching at the same time, synchronised with the rest of the platoon's marching. In this way the chest was twisted, distorted, warped and wrenched until the body was moving in one direction, the head facing another and the rifle out on a limb taking account of wind-blow! One might be forgiven for calling this Skill at Arms, but the instructors would be *seriously* upset, as this particular subject involves the use of the weapon in order to kill or, in my case, to hit the target. Dave Thomson, being born to the life of a Scots Guardsman, was extremely good at drill and looked a likely contender for the Sword of Honour. Tall and immaculately turned out he looked every bit the perfect Guards Officer after only six weeks.

Drill parades did seem somewhat irrelevant to our military careers, as we marched continuously round and round the Square; after all it took us away from the delights of the classroom discussions and a range of possibly enlightening exercises! It did however show the public face of the discipline and teamwork that are essential to any soldier. The Adjutant was particularly keen on drill: 'the bread and butter of the Guards', and rode around on horseback, bagging anyone who looked at him. What was 'reality' to the Colour Sergeant was torture to us. But the Adjutant had to have his fun. Our uniform had to be 'gleaming' everyday — and woe betide any man who was not up to scratch:

"You're in bog order man! Lock him away Colour Sergeant!"

"Yes Sir!"

Even the Standard Bearers received an earful:

"You're the biggest bunch of wimps I've ever seen!" the Adjutant bawled as a gust of wind caused the Standards to drop ten degrees from vertical.

At about this time the First Aid Course began. There was an intriguing dialogue on all aches and pains a body can feel; apparently "it's *pretty grim* if the breathing stops"!

Amongst many other aspects, we were taught how to stop the tongue bleeding. This was achieved by applying 'judicious pressure' to the tongue and was promptly followed up by a forced diet! I also learnt how to survive and fight in a Nuclear or Chemical climate and spent many happy (?) hours running around in a rubber suit called Noddy! This is an experience I thoroughly recommend for those who travel to the south of Spain every year to boil in their own sweat!

All these aspects of training prepared me for the inevitable Exercises. The first real *exercise* was a thirty-four mile forced march called 'Long Reach'. Within my highly motivated team of five, I prepared the maps and took measurements meticulously before packing spare clothes and rations inside my webbed belt. Naturally we could not start on an empty stomach, so we sat down and had a civilised meal at the side of the road while we waited for the 'green light'. No-one had remembered the tablecloths, but it did not seem to matter: no-one had remembered the tables! En route there were a number of command tasks to perform and my group had the dubious pleasure of assembling rifle parts in a dark tent, blindfolded. This was accomplished with a task leader shouting out instructions, while the rest of us passed rifle parts to the left and gun parts to the right, ending up with a selection of weapons that would more or less work, before the time ran out. As the sun ducked behind the horizon, we strode westwards, along the great rolling hillsides of the South Downs. After about twenty miles our conversation ground to a halt as we withdrew into our private thoughts and dissipated our energy in keeping up the pace, interrupted by the occasional grunt as a falling star or the whiff of anti-midge spray from a flank took our attention. By the time we reached checkpoint D we had travelled over thirty kilometres and were all physically exhausted: mentally we were 'in neutral'. Grinding out some energy from the reserves, we set to work on the second command task — First Aid. I was in charge of the casualty, who had apparently broken his leg. While Justin bound and insulated him, Rob and Tony brewed cups of hot chocolate and I gave all the reassurance I could think of. Simultaneously there were various signals that had to be encoded and sent by radio. Tony encoded these numerically; I re-encoded the numbers into letters and Justin sent them over the radio, which Rob carried.

When the chores had been satisfactorily accomplished, there was time for a wash and shave. With seven hours in which to complete the final fifteen kilometres, I kept the pace down. In this way we preserved enough energy for the two mile run at the end and also kept an hour in hand to tidy-up for the morning inspection. At checkpoint E a happy looking Colour Sergeant donated a seven foot log to us, which had to be carried to the next checkpoint two miles away, as his landrover had mysteriously broken down. Justin, who was both the tallest and the broadest of us, decided that this was just the thing to remove the itch from his shoulder: he picked it up, swung it around as if it was an overgrown matchstick and yomped off across the valley, to the cries of "easy!" and "why do they give us such simple tasks?"

Winning Squad: Exercise Longreach. The author is in the centre.

The penultimate task was initiated after an inspection. I was given a pile of sheets, each asking questions about a different aspect of military knowledge. Sitting everyone on the ground in a circle I handed one sheet to each member of the team to fill in all the answers he knew, before circulating the paper clockwise. When our time limit was up we had managed to answer most of the questions correctly and guess the rest. The Officer in charge lined us up for the final run in to the finish and radioed through the countdown. To say the last two miles were painful would be an unforgivable understatement. We had decided to go all out for the record, to set a precedent for future victories...besides which the Staff were known to be more lenient on the Drill Square if *their* platoon was beating all the others! We left the firewood at checkpoint F and sped off with blistered feet towards the finish line. I took two of the rifles to enable everyone to stick to the set pace and charged down the hillside to the half way point. Justin let fly a few prize comments, by way of encouragement and self-motivation, and Rob and Tony sprinted off to take a leading position. The last member of our team sped through the finish line at a time of twenty minutes, five seconds — five seconds off the record, but beating all the other sections in the course of it.

The journey back was excited and full of the sense of achievement. There was a weekend leave coming up and everybody had intricate plans on how to spend it. It took little time to dissemble the kit...we were all in a rush to go...

CHAPTER SIX: ADVENTUROUS TRAINING

The Glorious Twelfth was a good day for travelling — torrential rain poured down all day. The mountain train to Fort William was slow and uncomfortable, with no views to preoccupy me. The group of twelve was formed from an amalgamation of Officer Cadets from different Companies. Most of us had applied for the more recreational options, such as canoeing, riding or skiing. Some had gone on exchange visits to West Point in America or Offizier Schule des Heeres, Hanover, West Germany. Crispin Swayne had led an expedition to the Grand Canyon and other expeditions had been planned to Southern Spain, Gibraltar and Honduras. So it was with a touch of bitterness that we disembarked at Fort William, wrapped up in anoraks and looking a picture of misery!

We were met by two colourful Sergeants, who introduced themselves as 'Paul' and 'Tony', our course instructors. Rumour soon circulated that Paul, who was built like Charles Atlas — only smaller — was on holiday from the S.A.S. and Tony told us that he had been borrowed from the Royal Marines. Certainly they both looked the part, with bulging biceps and expressions which make Mad Max and Arnold Shwarzenegger look both tame and endearing! The rest of us looked like something out of a James Herbert novel, with glazed eyes and expressionless faces.

Two weeks of hill-walking, rock-climbing and camping lay before us. The first three days were spent getting to know the ropes, beginning and ending with lectures. The bulk of the time was spent rock-climbing and abseiling, rotating from safety supervision to climbing, with some moral support thrown in by Paul and Tony at opportune moments. From time to time we were visited by Senior Officers, which stimulated a certain amount of macho heroics, culminating in the rapid rope descent of the 'A' team singing "Jerranimoah!" in mid flight!

Having grasped the basics of climbing, we set forth on a navigational exercise. This was much more of an invigorating pursuit as we had complete command of the section for long periods of time and experienced the problems of instilling confidence amongst a group of similarly qualified men. The importance of this became even more apparent to us when the mist came down and we stumbled across the moors in single file, following the compass needle. Luckily, no-one lost the way. We arrived at our rendezvous in good time, glad to have achieved our task correctly.

The strict rules of Sandhurst were cast aside and a synchronised craze for hair ensued. Our cropped hair slowly grew back into shape and one or two beards sprung up in preparation for the summer recess. Gradually, military jargon dropped out of conversations and a touch of Scottish accentuation crept in. There were few pubs in Ballachullish, but we were well received wherever we went. Before long, we had acquired a taste for the local whiskies, which had a fine peaty flavour. The locals took great pride in their habitat, making splendid allusions in their descriptions of nearby landmarks and recalling their own wartime adventures. It was tremendous seeing the whole community gather in the pub; old couples drinking Scotch with us, younger men and women recounting their daily chores, all as if there wasn't a complaint to be voiced. These were proud people who vowed they would never take pensions or charity if it was offered, though we were told "an honest face is always welcome".

The second week was exhilarating. As the sun burst through the clouds in full glory, we drove north to Dundonnel by landrover. There was hardly a house to be seen. The road swept round lochs and through coastal glens, along the seashore and back into rocky countryside. A hundred miles around the coast was inches on the map and we covered quite a few inches. I was given the task of leading my section of five through the beautiful, but barren glens of the Northern Highlands, on the first day of a three day hike. We had one day of particularly hot sunshine, when we took to the water and swam in the freshwater loch beside our tents. We suffered the traumas of the hot weather too — we were attacked by swarms of midges. By morning there were thousands of little black bodies lying on the floors of our tents. Hot army tea and fried baconburger soon awakened us into activity. Our next camp was by the North Minch coast, twenty miles away. We washed our midge-bites remorsefully, packed up our 'force-ten' tents and swept the area of rubbish.

We had introduced ourselves by Christian names, as surnames were too complicated to remember over such a short course, but by this stage our Sandhurst-designated nicknames were in widespread use. Thus Smidge, Wacky, Spike and Lobo became common terms of endearment: Smidge was a small, unassuming character who darted around the place with a wicked grin on his face — he was the practical joker of the group. The night before he had torn apart hundreds of midges, which he presented to Tony for breakfast in the morning! Thus 'Sandwiched midge' became his nickname: Smidge. Spike was nicknamed, unoriginally, after his hairstyle, which now being unbrushed, was swept back over his head in the form of a spike.

'Lobo' was the least intelligent of the team, lacking even the smallest degree of common sense and this was explained away by Smidge as "the unfortunate result of a lobotomy in early life".

We set off from our lochside camp in teams of six, following Taf, who had been nominated leader for the day by Tony, and strode out into the wild chatting casually about an end of course party. After several miles the going became more difficult, with rocky sheen and areas of marsh. We broke into single file and plodded through silently. Lunch was eaten in a small stone shelter some travellers had built in the distant past, and we searched around vainly for signs of gaelic graffiti. The afternoon hike was easier going, and it was cooler too. Conversation turned to family and friends, hobbies and aspirations. We met no other hikers on our journey, indeed, the entire countryside was barren of life; just undisturbed rocks, patches of moss, heather and bracken interspersed with clear, freshwater lochs which glistened in the sunshine. Tony met us with the landrover at the side of the one and only road around the coast. He was sick of midges and proposed to camp by the sea where we could build a fire out of driftwood. With our total approval, Tony took the wheel and drove us to an area of sand that fitted our specifications exactly. He left us to find the other group and we busied ourselves putting up the tents on a flat area of grass a hundred yards from the road. Smidge and I went for a walk along the beach to find driftwood with the instructions from Tony that 'any stranded pools of trout we could find would add to the high esteem he held us in'! Here we met up with another group of tourists, Americans looking for the 'real' Scotland, and, calling the others to join us, sat down with them passing round their bottles of ten year old Laphroaig and several other Islay malts. In reciprocation we handed round our 'biscuits AB' and rations of fruit, exchanging adventures as the sun dipped briefly below the horizon. Tony explained that it was possible to see the sun throughout the night if the sky was clear, over the summer solstice.

Further North, right on the North-West tip of Scotland, we climbed the most northerly munro (mountain over 3000 feet high): Ben Hope. With our heads in the clouds and determined expressions on our faces we made a steady ascent to the summit. Here we discovered an old stone hut, still with a roof but looking as if it had seen better days. Sheltering from the gale we toasted The Queen, the instructors and the 'absent friends' we would shortly be visiting during the summer recess. Not wanting to hang around we descended rapidly, running down the hillside towards the awaiting landrovers with yelps of unOfficer-like 'halleluhas'. En route we passed seventeen frogs, three grouse, two deer, several thousand midges and a partridge in a spruce tree. The pathway was covered in boulders, interspersed with wild orchids and moss heather. The rain quickly evaporated filling the air with the pleasant scent of pollinating heather.

"Adventure training"

Back at Dundonnel, having finished cleaning and packing all the kit, we threw a party for the staff. Our cook dished up freshly smoked salmon and roast chicken: a vast improvement to the 'field conditions' rations of stew and tinned sausages! Some of us visited the pub to watch the Miss World Contest. Several pints later we bid adieux to the locals and returned to the hut where we discovered that party games were in progress. Challenges were being issued to one and all to imitate the instructors in a variety of games requiring technique and strength. These involved moving around a wooden chair without touching the floor, props or other people; and stretching out over the floor to place a can of beer as far away as possible with only one's feet touching the floor. This practice-balancing occupied several hours and our activities often ended with a resounding crash. Being a tough little fellow, Smidge was particularly good at the chair games, but it took a tall, powerful oaf like Lobo to win the brawn-requiring games on the floor!

Returning to Ballachullish, we completed the course tests, both theoretical and practical, involving rock-climbing, abseiling and 'leading expeditions' for a few miles of navigation. Without exception, we all came away with the Expedition Leaders qualification, qualifying us to lead our own soldiers on expeditions in the future.

"I can't understand it chaps, according to my
map the final check point should be here!"

CHAPTER SEVEN: DRAGON'S TEETH

The four hour journey to Sennybridge was uninterrupted except for a brief stop where seventy-two 'Big Macs' were ordered in five minutes. I read through the exercise outline (travel brochure?) on the way...Crispin pointed out that there was no mention of rain, cold, wind, premature rheumatism or mud, so we were in for a splendid holiday! He took up his mouth-organ and serenaded us into Sennybridge.

Wales was under a blanket of snow, which had drifted everywhere. We deliberated on whether the rifle ranges would be open — and whether the central heating was on! It wasn't: we froze. Except for a brief encounter with bayonets, there was little substitute for break-dancing on the snow! Crispin was on tremendous form. Looking like a cooler version of Mickey Rourke, with designer stubble and an ever-present grin he made the bayonet lunging look like something out of the 'Three Musketeers'! Coupled with the frenetic lunging, the sounds of Star Trek completed a magnificent display of eccentricity: enough to warm the heart, if not the body. Colour Sergeant Murray, as ever, rose to the occasion, delighting in showing us "how we in the Teeth Arms neutralise the bastard". Lessons had been well learned in the Falklands War and were passed on from our war-veteran instructors to us. We had been told that "one lunge is usually not enough to kill a soldier, you may have to bayonet him six or seven times before he is incapable of firing off at your back". Colour Sergeant Thomson had the last serious word of warning: "if there is anyone here who is not prepared to *kill* a man, faced in front of him, with cold steel, then you had better leave now..." No-one moved.

The Night Live-Firing Attack had been vetoed due to the appalling weather conditions, so we all slept soundly and were in relatively good order for the Training Exercises the next day. After a refreshing account of how to conduct an ambush, how to avoid being ambushed and how to counter-attack during an enemy ambush, I was given the task of commanding my platoon around a circuit of ambush positions, mounted up in 4-ton trucks. The procedure was rehearsed thoroughly, using the truck in the best way for the protection it offered: kneeling uncomfortably below the thick steel sideboards. With the help of a few hints from Captain Sexton, I managed to predict the likely ambush spots from my map and visualise how I should cope best. I gave a brief set of orders and we moved off in convoy. As soon as the enemy opened fire on us everyone sprinted into their pre-designated positions. With good covering fire going in the entrenched Nepalese from Moore's 'three section', I was able to move my assaulting sections to a flank and crawl up to within twenty feet of the enemy machine gun. Colonel Nason shadowed me throughout the move, watching my every movement and listening to the orders I whispered into the microphone of my radio:

"HELLO ONE TWO, THIS IS ONE ZERO, ATTACK ON MY WHISTLE, OUT".

As our grenades went off, I blew a shrill whistle blast and sprang up to assault, with five men on either side. The Gurkha soldiers, being well versed in 'how to die when an Officer Cadet shoots you', jumped in the air, twisted and turned to the tuneful rendition of "aaaaaargh!" and play-acted dead.

"Grab their machine gun and turn it on that machine gun nest to the left, Rob" I instructed, hurtling myself on to the ground as another burst of fire opened up. "Take that as read, Salvesen, and carry on without it" ordered Colonel Nason.

"ONE SECTION COVERING FIRE, TWO SECTION GO!" I shouted, struggling to my feet and chasing down the hill. "DOWN! ONE SECTION GO!" One section charged down the hill as we gave covering fire.

"STOP!" shouted Colonel Nason as the Gurkhas jumped to their rehearsed death, "Back to the vehicles for a debrief".

I led my assaulting sections back to the 4-ton trucks at a jog. Tony Moore's section had beaten us to it, sitting in a semi-circle on the roads.

"Good attack, Salvesen, though I felt you could have used the track behind that hedgerow to form up on. Well done on the radios, remember, good communications is the key." Colonel Nason concluded. Captain Sexton quickly appointed Tim Jones to clear another machine gun nest, which was irritating him, on the convoy circuit before lunch.

That was to be my only major command appointment of the exercise. That afternoon Jess took over command for some intricate House-clearing operations, described by 'Colour' as 'Domestic bliss'!

"Whatever you do, don't forget to knock!", he added, demonstrating with a thunderflash.

The whole operation ran smoothly, with everyone doing their damndest to impress the Directing Staff. Using ropes, ladders and second floor windows we assaulted the various 'terrorist occupied houses' that we were led to. Crispin Bond had found his niche. As a down-to-earth former soldier, he appreciated the finer qualities of 'minimum force', bursting the General

Purpose Machine Gun into maximum overdrive at the least provocation. "Never trust a politician", he muttered, adjusting his headdress and moving on to the next good cover.

Jess led the move-out that evening too. We trudged through mile after mile of snow towards a steeply inclined forest, which was to become home for the next few days. The descent into our new quarters was extremely hazardous, with ice and snow causing a mass of unrefined 'ski-bumming' incidents. I did suggest at the time that it would be much easier on skis, but the idea was abruptly shelved.

Day merged unobtrusively into night. The dish antennae of the radio station lost their dimensions in the dim light and appeared as black-inked thumb-prints above the skyline. I spent a few hours digging my shelter bay, creating an horizontal surface on which to sleep. Further through the night I dug the Base latrine, complete with chain and instructions! I was on sentry duty in the early hours with Taf, an easy-going Welshman of mining stock. As one of us lay out in the shelter bay beyond the perimeter, the other dug a defensive trench. Swapping over at twenty minute intervals, we managed to stay awake and warm as well as guard the Base. By dawn the trench had been completed by our respective 'reliefs' and we spent the early morning contemplating a colour coordination for the interior; putting in double glazing; hoovering the floor and applying for a home-improvements grant!

The completion of the Base was met with applause from the Company Commander (who was "just trying to keep warm") and a new set of Command appointments. The Company Sergeant Major proposed that "Mr. Halsey will now become 3 i/c to the 2 i/c of the C.P.", which graciously released him from hypothermia: the Command Post was a heated room in a Nissan hut. Meanwhile Reg, who was only blessed with the command of a reconnaissance patrol, was heard to enquire:

"When will I give the orders — before or after I go out?" which was greeted with raucous laughter.

Whenever the cold started to numb our spirits, there was always a ready wit to entertain us. Instead of a fitness run, in memory of the physical training staff, we created a brief Disco Dancing Championship. This might even have been achieved with a grimace were it not for the fine fettle of Crispin and Richard, who preferred to waltz, and looked like a couple of grisly bears at a circus, supporting their 'designer stubble'!

The daytime 'Fix and Destroy' operations passed by uneventfully with Gurkhas dying at their own discretion; and with patrols and ambushes keeping us on our toes there was little time for despondency that night. Plans were already afoot for larger operations and, after another day of hounding the small fry enemy, we covered our tracks and moved out. Carrying the General Purpose Machine Gun (Jimpy) I went on attachment to the Fire Support Group. We had a short, freezing march to a long ridge position,

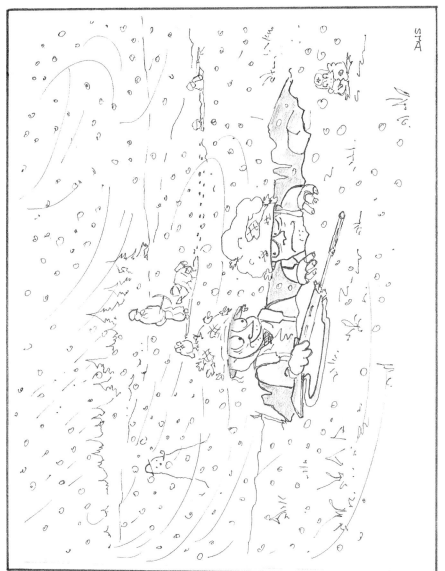

"Cedric I am really looking forward to Christmas"

from where we could all see the main enemy camp. And there we lay until dawn, silently watching layers of ice form on our boots; huddled in a long line of nonchalant misery and chattering teeth, within earshot of the enemy. It was my job to initiate the entire attack, as I had guaranteed that my gun would fire properly, without a stoppage. The Fire Support Group commander tapped my shoulder. Taking careful aim I unleashed a volley of blanks, shuddering the peaceful hillside and precipitating a rattling thunder of gunfire. This was supposed to continue in full effect for ten minutes, but due to the shortage of ammunition most of the firers had to resort to vocal support: it can only be assumed that our Gurkha antagonists died of hysteria! The attack went in and we had a theatre (of war) seat, similar to that of television viewers watching the Falklands War documentaries. Our advancing troops over-ran the Gurkha positions and "Endex" was called.

We were thoroughly debriefed on the enemy position while breakfast was set up before a wash, shave and kit check. A video film had been made during the exercise, which we were to see later. "In retrospect", Major O'Bree commented, "the weather was unseasonably good!" Our foreign students shivered audibly and we boarded the buses, grateful for the pre-meditated sleep that was to be taken on the journey back to Sandhurst.

All the weapons had to be thoroughly cleaned and inspected before they could be handed back into the armoury, not least the machine guns, which took the longest time to clean. After cleaning our own rifles and oiling them up, we shared out the pieces of each machine gun, the lightweight anti-tank weapons and all other weapons we had been using and set to with gritted teeth. We put a radio on to cheer us on our way and Colour Sergeant Thomson dropped by just in time to check the weapons, accompanied by his son, who was fascinated by such an exhausted array of grimacing soldiers.

We had previously chipped in to purchase an industrial sized washing machine for the platoon, which meant that we could wash our clothes in the Platoon lines and not face the long walk through New College to the Laundrette. On a rota basis, rotating clockwise by room numbers, one of us would be in charge of Platoon washes each day, leaving time in the evenings for personal items to be cleaned. Returning from exercise, clothes were hung on the hooks outside the door to be collected by that day's washer. Half the Platoons' combat shirts could be fitted in one wash, though only a section's worth of the heavier camouflage trousers could be managed. While the machine was set spinning, everyone rushed for first place in the showers, as there were only two baths in the lines. I was lucky in that my room was opposite the entrance to one set of the showers and one of the baths, so I nearly always made it to a bath before anyone else. On this occasion my body had been so numbed by the chill of Sennybridge that it took an hour before I felt freshened up, and by that time I had fallen asleep.

CHAPTER EIGHT: THE SAUSAGE MACHINE

Revived by the Bordeaux of the Academy Leave Weekend, I was in fine fettle for the programme of barrack lessons. The Company Commander entertained us all with an 'open forum' lecture on 'Leadership and Integrity'. Many of the expected quotations were voiced, giving Montgomery and Churchill a hitherto unrecorded Scots accent! The seriousness of the topic was not lost: Tony gave a colourful insight into the mistakes he had experienced form the Officers when he was a Private soldier; the Company Sergeant Major touched on examples of good leadership from his experiences in Northern Ireland and our Colour Sergeant inspired us with his account of the Falklands War. It was never far from my mind that, however much we liked or disliked our instructors, these men speaking to us were the cream of the British Army: the best instructors selected from thousands of Officers and Non-Commissioned Officers, regardless of Regiment or Corps. They were the leaders; we were merely students, hoping to emulate them, perhaps even to do better. We all had the *potential*, but it had still to be fully cultured.

Our own views on Leadership were not hidden either. Over the past few months we had each chosen an historic leader on whom to base a short lecture, at the end of our 'Communications Studies' package. This fulfilled a number of worthwhile aims: our own research had built up our understanding of what makes a leader and what makes a leader fall; our ability to construct and convey a lecture to a group of like-minded men was tested and our communication skills were tested still further by their effects on our fellow Officer Cadets and the staff.

My own lecturette was a serious historic look at Montgomery, based on his achievements and included BBC tape-recordings of two of his speeches and a set of illustrating slides, culminating in a list of what I considered to be Montgomery's leadership qualities and weaknesses.

Several members of the platoon made whopping historical errors; most of us merely encrusted our own views on our chosen characters. Churchill was described as "a well-known figure for his leadership potential"!

Apparently this "musical Winnie", whom most of us thought of as a hero, "concentrated on the essentials and buggered the rest." Tim went on, adding that "little needs to be said about the mans's self confidence — he was oozing the stuff!"! Later on we were told that "Hitler had the right aim — he wanted to rule the world"!

Most of the lectures were brilliantly put over with amateur theatricals. All manner of props and costumes were used, including plastercast boats, films borrowed from museums, slides and pictures. Crispin Bond came in dressed as a pirate to describe Captain Hook as "one-eyed Jim.....because there's only one 'i' in Jim!"

Atmospheric pressure became a theme, with a pirate fight using wooden swords, and water machine guns casting new light on the adventures of Sir Francis Drake. Several guys had taped 'battlefield interviews' with the help of local Jocks (Scottish soldiers) and a tape recorder on the Rifle Ranges! Indeed some had so much artistic licence that history became an excuse for a story! Mountbatten's battleships sunk in a sea of red herrings!

Sword Drill started with a flourish. Our Scots Colour Sergeant relished his moments of Drill and was in a particularly good mood. Non-Commissioned Officers are not normally trained in Sword Drill, so Colour had been on a few training sessions himself, prior to training us. Consequently the College Adjutant gave us an introduction, emphasising the necessity of perfectly synchronised movement and style. When Colour took over, he grinned triumphantly, flourished his sword into a gust of fresh air, and announced with equal relish....."Then you *waste* the guy!" Running commentary was an integral part of every Drill period, breathing new life into aching limbs, and this was no exception. After an hour or so of serious practice, in which most of our forage caps were knocked off, we marched back to the armoury in time to Colour's "Left ....Right..... Hop.....Skip.....January....February....March ....Right...."!

There was a Signals Exercise before lunch. Coupled with an orienteering competition, we shouldered our radios and sped off into the woods of The Barossa Valley. Unlike the vineyards of Australia, Sandhurst's Barossa is a vast area of hardwood, intertwined with new plantations of Sitka Spruce and webbed with paths. This has the effect of making map-reading extraordinarily difficult, though by this stage we were all familiar with the landmarks. Arriving at a given map coordinate, we proceeded to encode and send the radio messages which we found at the base of a tree or fastened to a gate post. The Signals staff at the Control Point took down the messages, which were marked later, and gave us further instructions, such as changing the frequency or decoding a further message to send over the air in plain English. The exercise went so predictably that after managing the first few messages without any difficulty, an attitude of 'let's beat them at their own game' was adopted and half the platoon ended up in the NAAFI drinking

3 Platoon after the log race.

P.T.I. Smith.

tea and intercepting radio messages which were sent several seconds later!

The Barossa Valley has seen many an adventure explode into creative mirth, though some exercises had become grim psychological traumas. It was in the Barossa that we learnt basic tactics on platoon exercises and it was in the Barossa that we developed our fitness.

Recapturing the atmosphere of arduous log races and sprints up Sirmoor Hill could not be achieved without mentioning the Physical Training Instructors. These are a rare breed of extremely fit men with a grotesque love of stamina. PTI Smith was one such character who lived up to the reputation of being 'a fair man'. Almost every day, when we were not on exercise, Staff Smith would set off with us, circumnavigating the 1,700 acres of Sandhurst training area. His sense of duty was there for all to see; working to 'get us through' with as little friction as possible. His authority was personal and our reward to him was to do our damndest in all the physical competitions. We even volunteered to spend several evenings before the 'march and shoot' and 'log race' in rehearsals, and Staff Smith in turn would give up his free time running with us. We ran from New College through the Barossa to the rifle ranges, which still smelt of cordite: shooting only seemed to stop for the Queen's Flight! We ran the full distance of the course including the assault course and by the end felt confident in our ability to win. It boosted our morale when we did win, there could be no greater reward for Staff Smith than that he had seen us doing our best, but we had added the icing to the cake.

On most runs he would ensure we ran our hearts out. Huffing and puffing we would be led through the woods carrying a degree of weight which gradually increased as we built up stamina. Discipline for the most part was self-inflicted though if anyone were to hold up the squad, he would be admonished by the others and dragged along. If there was any difference between the British and the overseas Officer Cadets it was will-power. This became apparent in any number of platoons in the succession of stretching runs. As the exercise became more demanding one or two foreigners in each platoon wilted in contrast to the British bulldog perseverance. To earn our respect the overseas students had to be better than us, if they faltered they condemned their race. On long forced marches we would take it in turns to call out a paced time, but we never sang. The British Army doesn't sing on the march; that went out with National Service. It was often on these long runs and marches that a man was "made or broken". There was no bullying or sympathy; it was a matter of guts. By this stage in the course those who were to fall by the wayside had left. The overseas Officer Cadets had little choice in the matter — as ambassadors to their respective countries they *had* to stick it out, so the less fit ones plugged along and caught up when we changed from a run to a marching pace.

On one occasion, suffering from the hangovers of a platoon party the night before, we were scheduled to start the morning with a two hour run in 'skeleton order' (minimum fighting gear). There was only a History lecture to follow and we were all looking forward to the long weekend ahead. John 'Mac' MacLean had reported sick that morning, with a 'strained ankle', which was unusual in that he never wimped out of runs, though as a Beagler he did the minimum possible afternoon exercise. Staff Smith hardly noticed his disappearance and we set off on our customary run through the woods, moaning inwardly. After about fifteen minutes casual jogging Staff Smith disappeared through a gap in some undergrowth and we followed through to an open clearing next to a rough muddy track. Imagine our astonishment when hurtling through the woods came Mac in his small estate car smiling mischievously! He ground to a halt, opened the boot and assembled crate after crate of beer, complete with table and white cloth!! Staff Smith had risked his career and arranged a tremendous party!

It was against the rules for us to thank the Directing Staff (D.S.) for all the hard work that they put in with a financial reward, but as the course progressed we felt it imperative that our Colour Sergeant should be rewarded. Mick Gallagher and Crispin Bond held 'platoon conflabs' and we resolved to send Colour Sergeant Thomson and his wife to Paris for the weekend, while Mick and Mrs Gallagher looked after their son.

We managed to escape for the weekend as well as our planned guard duties had been swapped with another platoon after the girls had been spotted in their lines. Even the plea of 'tea and biscuits' was rejected by the Company Sergeant Major!

CHAPTER NINE: WHITE KNIGHTS

We were midway through the course and many of my platoon had established relationships with available ladies who were invited to Sandhurst parties. Generally, these bore no relation to our backgrounds as individuals, as by this stage we were moulded more or less as a single entity and competed with other platoons for the most attractive girls. The competition was shared amongst our partners too, and Eastbourne Ladies were regularly heard slagging off nursery nurses with base venom! Montesori teachers, Norlands nannies and Chiltern nursery nurses kept the mockery in house — as if Officer Cadets were interested in bringing up children — and were tormented by constant reminders of 'how easy it must be to pin a nappy in comparison to digging trenches'.

Sitting in a classroom in tracksuits bulling boots together and sharing experiences on the many and varied exercises had forced friendships upon us that might never have been created in another environment, and the competition for the most attractive girls was as much a battle of wits between Officer Cadets on a social basis, with metaphorical back-stabbing and witty retorts in exchange, as on an emotional one. As often as not the winner was decided between the men, though the girls did have *some* say in the matter!

Casual bets were placed on the progress being made and periods of grace were extended to competing friends:

"If you don't get anywhere within the week I'll take her off your hands!"

"Two weeks."

"Deal."

Some girls managed to go through a whole string of Officer Cadets in this way, without any knowledge that the present partners had been cordially invited to 'pit their worth' by their forerunners! There was disenchantment too, amongst the 'fairer sex'. One of the Winkfield ladies, who became a great friend during my irregular visits to the 'Slug and Lettuce', complained that "Officer Cadets only act like gentlemen in order to get us into bed". This certainly had a ring of truth to it, as weeks away on exercise without seeing girls took its toll on otherwise sturdy strands of moral fibre. It seemed that Sandhurst men only pursued the attractive girls who had few inhibitions! However there was a branch of Potential Officers who were most certainly gentlemen, men who went into relationships seriously with a view to retaining their girlfriends for as long as they remained compatible. These were the 'white knights' of Sandhurst, predominantly Cavalry types, but with splatterings of corps and teeth arms as well. Most of these men had been brought up by the rules and intricacies of social etiquette and set high personal standards. If they had not chosen a career in the army, many of the Sandhurst gentlemen would have followed successful careers in the city, running their own businesses or as country gentlemen.

At a dinner party in Oxford, hosted by a fellow Officer Cadet one of the female guests drank some water out of her washbasin, which looked like an enlarged brandy glass! Unperturbed, my host did likewise and continued eating as normal, though his amusement was hard to hide! A less-feeling man would have pointed out the mistake and indulged in the embarrassment it caused.

It was about this time that Smidge jumped on the bandwagon and turned Green, which was ironic as Smidge had always wanted to fight in the Falklands, had he been around at the right time, and killing men seemed to me to be as anti-Green policy as killing seals, regardless of the motive. The stark truth of it was that Smidge was only half Green. Most of the time he was politically Blue; which made him a sort of turquoisy colour overall, with streaks of Red and White. Displaying a form of inverted snobbery, Smidge found it made him feel infinitely superior to criticize every well-meaning protester from the Greenham Common Women to the Aborigines in Australia, while in the same sentence uttering some loyalty to the basis of their protest. Thus references were made to CND's Rainbow Warrior circling Great Britain and annoying the dolphins, while proclaiming "save the shrimp, man!" in a loud sturdy voice: one could never be sure quite how sincere Smidge was. Like most Officer Cadets, Smidge loved the environment and spent much of his spare time at home gardening and planting trees. On the other hand he knew that if a swarm of Russians were charging across West Germany throwing handgrenades into the 'nuclear free zones', he would be quite prepared to send them home with an atom bomb singing 'O Flower of Scotland'. However, Smidge's Green approach had the novel effect of attracting one or two desirable young ladies in the Slug and Lettuce, which gave him the desired 'street cred'.

Amongst my brothers-in-arms were both the 'charmers', smooth talking and dominating every conversation and the 'loners', set apart but listening intently, every now and then adding a well calculated comment to the military banter. 'Integrity' was the name of the game and one's word became a bond, upheld as a 'matter of honour'. It was often impossible to spot a 'white knight' amongst a group of coupled Officer Cadets. The stimulating mental percussion could as often come from a self-confessed cad, like Smidge, 'whose wit was as fast as his women!' More often the gentlemen would be found 'hacking out' before a Beagle ball, hosting a party of outside friends. The border line between gentlemen and cads was made even more difficult to graph when into the throng came the mixtures, who would pick and choose their moments when to be upstanding and when to be lice. Gentlemen became passive creations: someone could not make himself a genuine gentleman, it was just the way he was; likewise he could not be a cad. And so it was left up to the girls to make up their own minds.

It was often easier to distinguish different standards of refinement in the field, where conversation degenerated to military phonetics and cliché; and from there to cursing. Here culture, courtesy and education were all hidden beneath the layers of 'cam cream' and foliage. Away from the ties of social protocol, pretence was abandoned and friendships died. Under the intense pressure of command it was remarkable how many true colours were exposed and we all said things we would rather not have. But the field was, by nature, an uncivilised environment and our own psychological warfare ruled our better intentions.

Conversation had been distorted on our arrival at Sandhurst and was now mottled with clipped speech. Acronyms took the place of nouns; jargon became universal. Even debriefs used an economy of words — heaven help the individual who had to give a blow by blow account! We talked about documents by their military numbers, mixing the terminology with dates of famous British victories, phonetic dialogue and quotations from our Oath of Allegiance, until it became so meaningless to an outsider that partners often accused Officer Cadets of 'white lies'! Charging around Salisbury shouting "right flanking attack!" and "form up at the FRV; Sunray will sign the ten-sixty-six and we'll blow out Texas. We then move into phase five, the move back to RV with two zero at Whisky Tango", was a bewildering experience that became second nature. Captain Sexton was more poignant on the subject, citing a wise commander who observed "show me a (complete disaster) and I'll show you a break down in communications!" and with that went "Oscar Uniform Tango".

CHAPTER TEN: BATON ROUGE

The Counter-Insurgency Exercise started in earnest, after a tremendous series of lectures and demonstrations, at Longmoor Camp. With Royal Marines and W.R.A.C. privates trained in rioting, acting as the enemy, our task was to restore law and order to the town and its surrounding area. Rumour Control (those with black market knowledge acquired from previous courses) predicted that each platoon would face two 'soft' riots and two of the 'hard' variety, in a reconstruction of the disturbances in Northern Ireland: the Exercise was not directly related to Northern Ireland, but had many similarities. Certainly, the urban environment confirmed this predicament, though the passage of events was carefully controlled. My platoon went through the patrolling part of the Exercise last, so the rioting crowds had worked up some adrenalin by the time we saw them.

Rounding a street corner we saw a mass of men and women building a barricade across the road. Simultaneously, they saw us. With a cry of "Take cover!", we beat a hasty retreat, dodging the hail of rubber tyres and petrol bombs that were hurtling towards us. Reinforcements were quickly assembled and, protected by anti-riot shields and helmets we approached the barricade. We were formed up resembling an armadillo, reminiscent of the siege warfare of the Crusades. Well versed in the theory of riot control, we attempted to persuade the crowd to disperse, using a megaphone. This was closely followed by the threat of violence, when burning rubber was thrown at us. We marched towards the crowd, firing blank plastic bullets at the main agitators and pulling parts of the barricade apart. Suddenly, there was a shrill whistle blast. The crowd rapidly dispersed. A shot rang out; a terrorist marksman was firing at us. Briefed by one of the instructors, Charlie fell down to the ground, squealing for help. There was a sudden panic as we dropped our riot shields, unstrapped our rifles and took cover, looking for the gunman. George spotted a man running from one of the buildings, carrying a rifle. Shouting out directions, he rapidly gave chase, followed by his section. My section ran around to the house the rifleman had run from, to cover George and protect any forensic evidence. There we

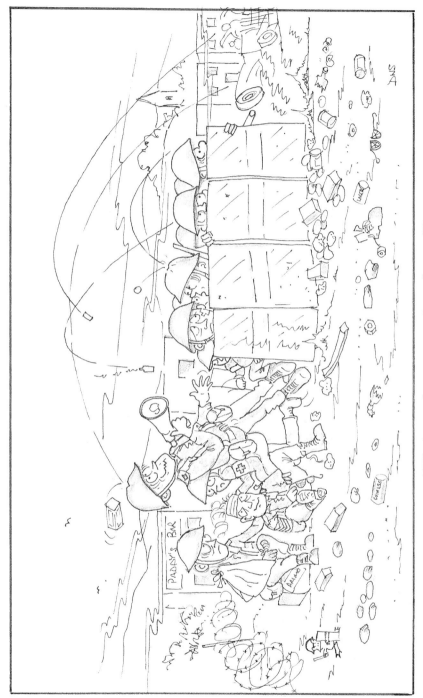

"Who's next for a command appointment?"

found a couple of terrified hostages bound up. I quickly unbound the nearest of them and flung us both out the door as he shouted out "Booby Trap!" Man-handling the couple to safety, we cordoned off the house, summoning extra help, reporting the situation over the radio as we moved around.

Luckily, George, who was built like Arnold Schwarzenegger, had caught the gunman, who had surrendered — throwing the rifle away in terrified panic. Chris' section had summoned an ambulance for Charlie, who was acting unconscious. They found some witnesses at the barricade and took them aside for questioning. The forensic experts arrived some time later to assess the booby trap, which was blown-up, and George's section found the terrorist rifle in the nearby graveyard. It took a considerable time for the forensic experts to finish off, but we were all too busy questioning pedestrians and keeping the 'civ. pop.' away from the forensics to notice.

We were given a major debrief on the merits and mistakes of our patrol, with a full video of the event, taken from one of the rooftops. The Company Commander was pleased with our first attempt, but pointed out that the 'real thing' is not nearly so straight forward!

My own patrol moved out to some exciting fun. As we wandered through the town, questioning shoppers and suspects about recent terrorist events, I received a radio report of a "suspicious device" outside the post office. Familiar to the lay out of the town, I moved my Section straight to the post office: we arrived so quickly that the Directing Staff had not put out the device when we arrived! This was soon put right and I carried out the appropriate procedures to cordon off the area and move out the residents living nearby. We had excellent communications and organised a control point and safety area within minutes. I had taken a close look at the device through binoculars, to check that it wasn't a hoax and summoned our Technical Officer (alias the Company Sergeant Major) to conduct a controlled explosion.

Throughout the day we alternated from patrolling to guarding the base, with a little sleep in between, before going out in armoured cars (pigs) as the Quick Reaction Force. This was immensely exciting as we were taken directly to the thick of the trouble spots, psyched-up and alert. Major Lees controlled the exercise with a firm grip to ensure that no-one was hurt. Like the other Instructors at Sandhurst, he showed great patience. It was remarkable to see and understand how a few words from a great Commander can gain and retain the respect of so many men. Major Lees was one of those Commanders. He stood tall and lean, with a sandy moustache and had the ability to pick us out from a crowd before we made mistakes, ask what we were intending to do and set us on the right track. In this way, serious errors were ironed out before they became habit and we didn't feel we had done wrong. And if the 'enemy' made mistakes in their rioting, Major Lees would stop the Exercise, explain where it was going wrong and what ought to be happening in such a calm, professional manner that we all felt we had overcome great difficulties.

The final operation of the exercise was a pub clearance. This involved the entire Company. Our intelligence reports suggested that a terrorist conference was being organised at the pub, bringing the different terrorist factions together for an assault on the Base. The Officer Cadet in charge of the Company decided that this would be particularly dire, especially for the the platoon on Base Security. So we went into an overnight covert mode, surrounding the pub. The other platoons waited until we were in position, which took slightly longer than had been expected, and moved into the armoured landrovers.

One moment the stars twinkled like glow worms in a dark cave; the next, it was like fireworks night! Flares shot up all around the pub. Simultaneously, the armoured vehicles arrived and sixty Officer Cadets charged into the pub, bringing the occupants out into a long line by a predesignated wall. Some of the 'civ. pop.' tried to run away into the countryside but were quickly returned to the wall shouting abuse at their captors. After a long search, a collection of weapons and munitions was uncovered and the suspected terrorists arrested. The remainder of the 'civ. pop.' were searched and released with an apology.

The debrief was, once again, full of alternative methods of accomplishing the operation, but we were congratulated on what we had accomplished, with the promise of much more training prior to the real thing!

CHAPTER ELEVEN: QUEENSBERRY RULES

Sports formed an integral part of the Fitness curriculum, and consisted of two afternoons a week being spent pursuing a variety of sports. Those lucky enough to be picked for an Academy Team pursued their chosen sport without variety, often staying back at weekends to play matches rather than go on Leave. This could have its benefits as well as its penalties: Officer Cadets and Graduate Officers alike were frequently whisked back at the end of an Exercise in the Sports Officer's or Padre's Landrover to represent The Academy. Likewise it could mean being given better dates for Guard Duty, which meant less weekends spent checking identity cards at the entry gates or strolling around the Academy in uniform when everyone else was burning rubber to London. There were also a few main sports fixtures when the whole academy stood supporting on the touchline, adding to the feeling of achievement; even if the spectators were only there for the beer! Rugby and football were the main spectator sports, with cricket taking total dominance during the summer term: the queues for pints of Pimms outside the Quboos Pavilion bore testament to the game's attraction!

Those who did not play for the Academy or Company teams voted for what sports they would like to pursue and this was organised by the Company Colour Sergeants, providing there was sufficient demand (though occasionally a sport was chosen by the supervising staff and numbers were volunteered). For the less athletic there was always Beagling, while many Officer Cadets chose to play Tennis or Squash and escaped as quickly as possible to catch a train to London or go home for the evening. Most sports were catered for, including the oriental arts of Kung-Fu and Karate, which always had a popular following.

Swimming was taken seriously; not a pursuit for the casual swimmer! Ulterior motives were spotted at the Academy Swimming Championships when it was noted that "the costumes improved the girls' appearance enormously": the W.R.A.C. suddenly found themselves invited to every platoon party! Coupled with 'Watermanship', swimming could be an aggressive and exciting adventure. Watermanship was a new and savage exploit on the assault course pond. A volunteer was needed to swim and fetch the makeshift raft, which was tethered to a lump of concrete in the middle of the pond and I was flung into the water in the rush! However, as the Instructor pointed out, everyone would "get the opportunity to get wet sooner than you think!" I swum to the raft and towed it in, to the applause of the spectating rowers. After an hour or so of tuition in the military and safety aspects of assault craft, a competition was announced. This was "to test our speed and flexibility", we were informed. Four assault boats were lined up and we were split up into teams. We were to row to the other side of the pond while the other half of our team ran around the edge carrying large ammunition boxes containing bricks. At the other side we were to swap over.

The whistle blew and we sped off across the pond. As our running team-mates flung members of the opposing factions into the mud around the edge of the pond, we splashed our opposite numbers with water. When this failed to provoke their capitulation, we sped through the spray and pirated one of the other vessels, throwing its occupants unceremoniously into the cold, forbidding pond, whence to swim to shore. This in turn happened to us from the other flank, and we ended up third!

Not content with having soaked *most* of us, the Physical Training Instructors finished the session with the 'Death Slide'. Having climbed up one of the great oaks of Sandhurst to a height of over one hundred feet, we arrived in a queue at a man-made platform which held a commanding view of the lake. Between the northern and southern sides was strung a thin rope of burnished steel, which "may not hold out if you don't put your heart into it", we were told. Our Physical Training Instructor, PTI Smith, checked that we were correctly positioned on the hand-harness and with an encouraging "carry on soldier!" sent us flying down the slide towards the bank of mud at the other side of the lake. Determined not to show any fear of heights, most of us put Tarzan to shame, shouting out whatever macho phrases came to mind during the descent, though the well-worn "Jerrannnimooah!" was inaudible in the rush of air.

I was lucky enough to be chosen for the hockey team and spent many happy afternoons in the spring and summer chasing the ball across the pitch "like a Highland Terrier". Colour Sergeant Thomson took great interest in my progress and encouraged the Company to lend the hockey teams some support on Academy Sports Weekends. The Graduates joined in on the sports front, one of the few areas where we did meet in the working hours. The Womens Royal Army Corps Officers and female Officer Cadets were generally segregated, though we did join forces on the Hockey Pitch for the occasional mixed match.

As a consequence, a good deal of enmity built up between the Graduates and Non-Graduates, encouraged for its competitive aspects by the Staff.

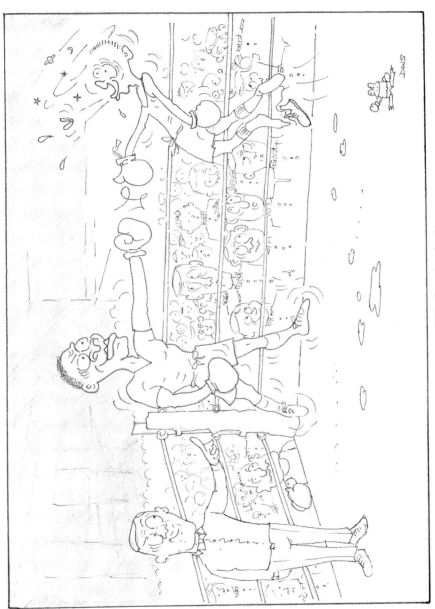

"Novices boxing"

The basis for this was that, though both graduates and non-graduates receive the same training and finish Sandhurst with the same military knowledge and ability, the graduates were to be promoted much more quickly, and paid more than their contemporary non-graduates both at Sandhurst and beyond. This has some sound reasoning behind it, but at Sandhurst it is considered by most students in both colleges as grossly unfair!

Bursting ferociously into the curriculum, the Inter-Company Boxing Championship loomed before us like 'Rocky V'. The main contests were between New College, the Standard Course, and Victory College, the Graduates. The gymnasium was transformed for the occasion, displaying all the trappings of a major sporting event. Attendance was compulsory, except for the W.R.A.C. Officers, who were not allowed to attend as it was decided that 'displays of gratuitous violence were not suitable for young ladies to watch'! The irony here is that some of the ladies who pass through Sandhurst are tough to the point of being Ramboesque! (though *most* of the ladies were sensitively feminine and would not appreciate such brutish sports!). Where Sandhurst glorifies the macho bulldog in the ring, the leaders in 'this man's army', it cultivates those ladies who are charming, intelligent and witty, yet thoroughly dedicated and professional. And it is no loss to the British army to boast of some very pretty female Officers indeed!

Dressed in our Sandhurst Blues, with highly polished shoes and bearing expressions of venomous apprehension, we gathered in the gymnasium; graduates on one side, non-grads on the other. The Band, borrowed from 1st Battalion, The Parachute Regiment, played in the Directing Staff. The Academy Sergeant Major, who had briefed us earlier to "sit to attention, with hands knuckled, one on either knee, and back straight", stood in the middle of the ring, saluted the Commandant, summarised the rules and introduced the first fight.

"Bout number one will be a Welter weight contest between....... representing New College and standing in the red corner, Officer Cadet Murphy and....... representing Victory College and standing in the blue corner, Second Lieutenant Whitworth.....". Each man stood to attention as his name was called amid the cheers of the supporting spectators.

The competitors had been picked over several months of milling and had been trained up by the Physical Training Staff during the sports afternoons and in the evenings. Most of the New College Team had had the previous toughening-up of Rowallen Company under their belts, so they were in even better shape than the rest of us. One or two had also been amateur boxers at school.

Throughout the fifteen bouts New College discharged volleys of violent blows on the Victory College opponents, egged on by the growing rapport with their supporters, These were actively opposed, but to little avail. The

Graduates fell asunder and the Judges found no difficulty in proclaiming New College the victors. The savage display of uncivilised brutality showed, conclusively, that convulsive temperaments and open aggression have a firm place in the Officer Corps.

The Commandant presented prizes to the winners of each bout and their concussed runners-up, and made a short speech about the guts of the competitors (one of the runners-up looked as if he was about to throw them out for inspection!), ending with the customary "Carry on Sergeant Major!"

CHAPTER TWELVE: PANACHE BRETON

A convoy of two companies of Officer Cadets, complete with pipers, logistic support and massed Directing Staff is difficult to disguise at the best of times. In this instance, given the high morale that a *final* exercise commands, no attempt was made. The journey from Camberley to St. Cyr, France, was consequently a proud and relaxed trip. 'Volunteers' from each platoon were posted to guard the weapons and ammunition (blank), while the rest of us congregated in the ferry bars, entertaining the other tourists.

The 'Ecole Speciale de Militaire de St. Cyr' is situated in the town of Coetquidan, near Rennes and trains Officers from all branches of the French Army. The most striking difference between Sandhurst and St. Cyr is that our French counterparts have all done their term of National Service prior to entering the school. Like the American system, the French Course is two years long and covers every aspect of low-level Military operations. At the end of their training at St. Cyr the newly Commissioned French Officers attain a degree in Military Studies.

In order to prepare the Exercise as thoroughly as possible the Directing Staff went into the field for a rehearsal, while we had two days in camp. As soon as we had unpacked, Number One Dress was put on and we marched onto the main square for a ceremony of welcome, which involved a great deal of coming to attention and standing at ease. In contrast to the bold orders of the Company Sergeant Major and Colonel Nason, the French Drill commands sounded like gentle requests: the Company Sergeant Major bawled out a tremendous volume of command, the French Commanding Officer simply spoke his commands! This was later explained as the reason for so many repetitions of basic drill movements: apparently the respective Commanding Officers could not believe the way their opposite numbers conducted his drill. Even more humorous to us, as we had not come across the phenomenon before, was the fact that our College Commander did not shout out the orders himself, but called out "Sergeant Major" whenever a drill movement was required. The Sergeant Major, being a wily man with a tremendous amount of grey matter, and an abundance of knowledge, which I was told was acquired from the Quarter Master's store, along with the extra pair of lightweight trousers, calmly took account of what the French had just done, translated it into British Military jargon and invariably blasted forth "Sandhurst, Saaaaandhurrrrst Shun!"

That evening we were divided up into sections and taken round to the accommodation blocks. The French 'Sous Lieutenants' lived in shared rooms of three or four during their first year, but graduated to single rooms in their second. This followed on naturally from their course of instruction, which was mainly physical in the first year and academic in the second. In contrast, the rooms at Sandhurst were single throughout, enabling graduates and Officer Cadets to study in solitude in the evenings. In the French rooms, away from the eyes of the Directing staff, bottles of beer were broken open and the welcome began in earnest.

A five course Dinner awaited us in the main Dining Room, complete with an array of specially chosen table wines and waiter service. The French were as inquisitive as ourselves, demanding comparisons to every aspect of training, short of breaking the official secrets Act (which covers just about everything!). Eventually we conversed our way to the Regimental System, which all of us going into Regiments (as opposed to Corps) were eager to defend. It soon became apparent that Johnny Findlay and I were particularly proud of going to Scottish Regiments. As this transpired the pipers we had brought along came into the room and we were challenged to prove our patronage. Nothing daunted, Johnny and I sprung up and, in a rapidly cleared place in the thick of the tables, reeled a mixture of the Foursome and Highland Fling in time to the pipes, whooping traditional Scots shrieks! This gregarious show of national pride caused a standing ovation, much to our embarrassment, and was quickly followed on by speeches from our respective Company Commanders; both in French, though translated through an interpreter for the less linguistic of us.

The French Army sing wherever they go and this was to be no exception. With synchronised harmony and a repertoire worthy of the Royal Academy the French broke into song. Not to be outdone, we had prepared a few harmonies of our own, but our forte was the hymn 'I vow to thee my Country'. It came roaring in nationalistic splendour as we stood to attention. Taking turns singing out our most patriotic songs, something of a contest soon evolved, and our volume control soon took command of the situation, for the harmony of the French military can never succumb.

Competitive spirit continued on the Saturday with a day of sports. The French had devised an array of competitions we could not possibly win! They chose the French assault course (quite different to the British variety), with its large concrete obstacles and seige wall; volleyball; handball; swimming; rugby on horseback and show jumping. We managed to retain our pride by winning the equestrian events and the volleyball, but were well

Professional progress in defence.

and truly thrashed in the other events, particularly on the assault course. There we raced more for each other's entertainment than for the trophy — the ultimate run of Thirteen Platoon's 'Who cares who wins' team turned the race into a spectator sport, capturing the attention of the most cameras!

The French saw us off with a fine Champagne cocktail party on Sunday morning, before we moved out into the field for ten days of Exercise. Final Exercises have had a tradition of being tremendous fun for both the Directing staff and Officer Cadets. In the field there has tended to be much less supervision than on any other Sandhurst Exercise, which makes for a more realistic exercise, and a big effort was made by the Quarter Master to supply a realistic amount of blank ammunition and pyrotechnics (in stark contrast to most other Army exercises, where ammunition is invariably in short supply).

'Panache Breton', however, started with a deliberate, serious and professional attitude. In my Platoon two of 'the lads' were still being assessed: the Directing staff were not finally decided on whether they were ready to hold a Commission, or whether they needed more time training. This meant that a watchful eye was kept upon us, keeping the pressure on the assessed. Coupled with the serious atmosphere, the clouds burst open and torrential rain poured down; apathy began to take a hold. Drenched and unhappy, we ploughed on, moving base three times the first day from wood to wood until we found out on the third day of the exercise, through radio messages, that the other platoons were spending the nights in barns! Eventually Colonel Nason ordered everyone into barns officially, in order to dry off. Reconnaissance patrols were dispatched to local shops and pubs (covertly!) and the composite rations were returned to the main Base! The radio message for "some ammunition, pyrotechnics, several vintage wines, some glasses and *more fun please!*" was sent with much scepticism, but the next day we locked up our rucksacks and went on a tour of the Battleground of Saint Marcel, the 1944 scene of one of the few pitched battles between the French Resistance and the German Wehrmacht.

Typically, an operation would begin with orders at sunset, sleep until 4 a.m., with a mad scramble to find boots and rifles in the dark, and onto the 4-ton trucks. At the Company Command post we waited several hours for helicopters, causing the Commanders anxiety as the dawn attack would have to be mounted in broad daylight. However, we found our positions correctly and with the minimum of fuss, launching a splendid assault at ten o'clock: the enemy died before they had time to drink their tea! We managed to return to our barn by mid-day, in time for an open air Good Friday Service. This was taken by Padre Brian and was a serious religious service which typifies the importance we placed on a religious outlook and sense of purpose: without such a committed sense of right and wrong there would only remain a nationalistic sense of 'The Just War', an attitude of 'My

Country Right or Wrong', which is no longer the case. Of course, the discipline remains, and the army would fight when and where it is told, but an inner feeling of fighting because it is the lesser of two evils would probably make combat easier to come to terms with. Not a man among us said he would not kill a legitimate enemy in a war situation; if we could not come to terms with *that* we would have no place in the British Army.

That night we held a Platoon party in one of the village pubs, hosting the Company Directing Staff. Like all parties at Sandhurst, the atmosphere of upright discipline is dropped, though the staff continue to be addressed by their rank out of courtesy and respect. On this occasion a few freudian slips added to the concourse as nicknames were shed upon the staff!

The Final Attack was brought forward a day. It is customary for Officer Cadets to wear their Regimental headdress for the first time on the Final Attack of the Final Exercise, and I donned my Tam O'Shanter for the first time with tremendous pride, though the Company Sergeant Major had occasion to describe it as a "helicopter landing pad"! I was a 'buckshee' machine-gunner in the reserve and would have had an eventless attack, were it not for Rumour Control, in this instance the staff, who passed the word that the enemy were preparing for a counter attack. All machine-gunners were summoned to 'the rock' where we poured blank ammunition into the retreating Gurkhas with great enthusiasm! Happily, the last retreating Gurkha obliged us and with a performance worthy of the Royal Shakespeare Company, threw up his arms and 'died' — magnificently!

"On exercise"

78

CHAPTER THIRTEEN: AN EYE FOR DETAIL

Dominated by endless inspections and long mornings of draining drill movements, the rehearsals for the Sovereign's Parade had an air of suppression about them. These were sober occasions in which every flicker of movement was observed; smiling was out of the question, as were tiny fragments of dust on the uniforms. Each night one or other of our uniforms were carried down to the dry-cleaners, paid for out of our earnings. Likewise, our boots were methodically bulled each night: dressed in tracksuits we spent hour after supervised hour rubbing polish and water in little circles on our drill boots, until our faces shone brilliantly in reflection. My forte was still belt buckles; polishing brass until the buckles shone more brilliantly than the boots. Invariably I would swap my boots for someone else's buckles, usually cleaning-up four or five pairs by the time my boots had been done. Besides rehearsing for the Parade itself I also had to rehearse the procedures for being presented to The Princess Royal. This was, by contrast, a pleasant set of rehearsals involving a quick chat with the Regimental representative, Colonel Watson, and the Commandant.

Preceding the Commandant's rehearsal, three days before the Parade itself, came the Adjutant's rehearsal. There was a great tradition to this occasion, coming as it did at the end of ten days of solid drill. The Adjutant's Rehearsal was the occasion in which each Platoon performs a skit in front of the other platoons. In the past, pre-planned heroics have been achieved, including the diversion of all the Camberley traffic through Sandhurst, in front of the Parade; the arrival of a mock Queen's convoy with professional actors and actresses playing the role of the Royal Family; the turfing over of the New College Parade Ground; the appearance of a Jolly Roger on the New College flagpole, and the kidnapping of the Adjutant's horse. Nowadays the skits are only slightly less heroic, with a ban on 'gross-o-grams' and an emphasis on 'good taste'; the Adjutant has a permanent guard on his horse at night!

For our skits we had summoned help from the Fire Service and Army Air Corps. The winners of the Sword of Honour and the Sash of Honour also

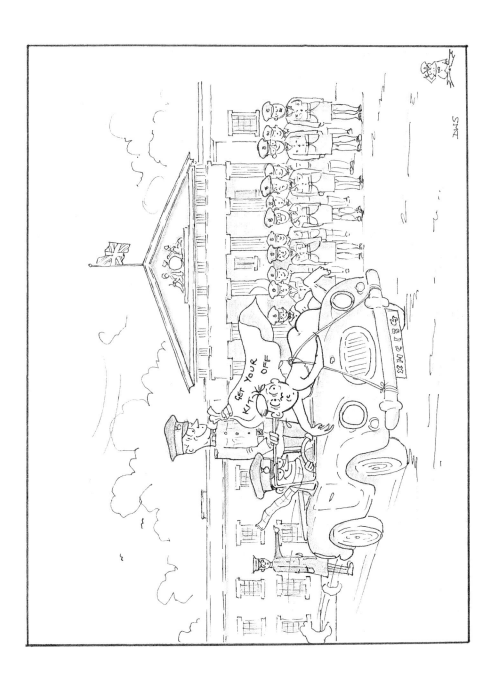

played their part. Using a number of smoke devices the appearance of a 'fire' in the New College buildings sent the parading companies into spasms of laughter. As members of my platoon abseiled down the side of the building, the cleaning staff let balloons out the top windows and cried out for assistance. The Fire Engine arrived much more quickly than anyone could have expected, raising a ladder to the bemused staff. At the same time the Sword and Sash of Honour winners were brought out in a bed, in front of the assembled multitude and an imitation of the Adjutant was performed; well performed mimics always receive the loudest applause! Meanwhile another platoon arrived in a topless bus with the band playing on the top deck! The girls were given the fright of their lives when a naked body, strung to the bonnet of an Officer-Cadet's car sped around in front of the Parade, before stopping sharply in front of their Company. A white flag, which had been draped across the body was raised, with the prayer 'Get your kit off!' written across it! The girls retorted with their version of 'Hey Big Spender' performed in split skirts and fishnet tights in front of everyone. Ultimately, a helicopter arrived and dropped off one of the Platoon Sergeants, dressed in his underclothes. He was duly marched up in front of the Adjutant with the explanation that he had been intoxicated and kidnapped the night before!

The fun and games over, the Adjutant proceeded in the orchestration of his rehearsal as if nothing had happened. We marched briskly from 'chaos corner' onto the revered Old College Square. Once there, we marched around and around the Square practising our drill movements and stood silently in the rain, presenting arms, while the Adjutant inspected everyone. As usual one or two individuals fainted, giving the Adjutant an excuse for revenge: a loud sermon followed by dispatching his unfortunate victims to the jail.

'Sergeant Major, who's that untidy man in the front row? . . . No, the next one along . . . Take his name! . . . You're a gorilla man! What are you? . . . Sergeant Major, fetch that man a gorilla suit! Gorillas should be kept in cages! Lock him away Colour Sergeant!'

Holding rifles out in front of your face for an hour is, at the best of times, a painful experience; in heavy wind and rain it was sheer misery. But a spell of sunshine took away the gloom and a synchronised humming of hymns, with individuals humming different instruments, took away the boredom. Inspection over, the Adjutant called in all the Company Sergeant Majors to reprimand them and explain the next half hour of rehearsal. The Sergeant Majors marched back into position and the Adjutant made a short explanatory speech to us, before marching us around the Square again. Eventually the Adjutant was satisfied and we finished the rehearsal in grand style, climbing the Old College steps in slow time, with the Band playing one of the Academy slow march tunes.

The chance of another, mixed party was seized. The Women's Royal

Army Corps held a 'Pub Sign Party' in the pavilion, with resplendent disguises, ranging from the 'Jolly Farmer', to the 'Slug and Lettuce' in a gesture of thanksgiving and of sentimental valediction. A fond farewell was also being sung to the much maligned Ladies of Winkfield, nursery nurses of Chiltern and Norland nannies in the Alamein lines. Used to the constant comings and goings of Officer Cadets, our partners and girlfriends were always aware that the final days of our Sandhurst Course could mark a severance of relationships. Only the strongest friendships remaining intact, where perennial partners are transformed into Regimental Groupees, sealed with an invitation to the Commissioning Ball.

As always the hosts and hostesses had grappled with the problems of entertaining in a unique and exciting way. Transforming the bland classrooms of Alamein has always been a cause for heartache, but the determination to impress and the sparkle of theatrical wit embodied in the Entertainments Committees shines through. Using the wealth of friends and contacts both within and outside Sandhurst, silk linings from the inside of parachutes were draped from the ceilings, discotheque lights installed and decorations hung in the manner of the themes. Catering was solved by a visit to the Chief Steward and a few drinks with the bar manager. With the stage set, convoys of Officer Cadets headed into Camberley to hire costumes. Manners in respect to looking after guests properly are never more apparent than at an Army party, where a competitive spirit is engrained in every aspect of behaviour. Vying for the attention of the opposite sex could be both spectacular and nimble-witted: using every twist and turn of insinuation, bantering repartee flew between groups of Officer-Cadets until the battle was won . . . or lost to all! By this stage in the course the girls were quite used to the army lingo and joined in with a vengeance, citing stories from exercises and past parties to infuriate the combatants often playing one man off against another for their own amusement. Revenge, it appeared, was sweet.

The Commandant's rehearsal, the next day, was a start to finish run through of 'the real thing', in our Khaki No.2 dress. Down at the pressers' 250 Sandhurst Blues were being dry cleaned in preparation. Most of us were wearing our second pair of bulled boots, leaving the best pair for that final glow parade boots are famous for. There was a final parade scheduled for the day before the Sovereign's Parade, but it had become established custom for the Commandant to be sufficiently impressed at his rehearsal as to cancel the last one, enabling us to prepare the uniforms properly.

CHAPTER FOURTEEN: MISSION ACCOMPLISHED!

The traditions associated with receiving the Queen's Commission kick off with the Commissioning Dinner: a large, formal dinner, which the Army had mastered to a fine art. Some of us had been chosen to host members of the Directing Staff and met up with our nominated guests in the New College bar. Pre-Dinner drinks were provided, relaxing everyone and we managed to keep most of the exercises out of our conversation. On this occasion I had no one to host, so I was able to catch up with the latest news. An absence of news, on the rare occasions there is a dearth, preceded a wave of gossip from 'Rumour Control', coupled with some psychic predictions on the most recent partnerships of Officer-Cadets with Winkfield Ladies, W.R.A.C. Officers or, less often, long-standing girlfriends. Prior to *my* Commissioning Dinner the conversation had been dominated by inquisitive rounds of 'who are you taking to the Ball?'

Dinner itself was a splendid affair, with sumptuous dishes served up in the candlelit environment of the New College Dining room. Silver was omnipresent, in magnificent arrangements celebrating past battles and Regimental victories. Each course was served with a different wine — glasses were never left empty. On completion of the fourth course, port was circulated, though left untouched . . . The President of the Mess Committee rang the small, silver bell beside him and stood up in the sudden silence, declaring in a loud, steady voice: 'Mr. Vice . . . The Queen!'

The Vice-President of the Mess Committee, a Cadet Under-Officer appointed to the position for the evening was sitting at the other end of the table. He stood up sharply, with a hint of nervousness, composed himself and toasted: 'Gentlemen . . . The Queen!'

Sudden commotion broke out as everyone rose rapidly to their feet. The Band played the National Anthem as we stood, stiffly, to attention. As soon as the final bar had been played, we all raised our port glasses and toasting 'The Queen!' sank the liquid down our throats with smiles of satisfaction. Shooting port was recirculated, along with cigars and cigarettes.

Quite unexpectedly, Colonel Nason rose silencing the chatter. It was quite unusual for a speech to be made after dinner, he said, but was driven to this exception to commend one of us present, who had added to his entertainment over the past months, by writing a journal, faulted only for its likeness to 'Tatler'. He went on to applause as I sat blushing, explaining that, while most Officer Cadets had filled two journal books with comments about our lives at Sandhurst, I had filled five! I rose to receive his presentation, proud in the receipt of such recognition.

At last the Commissioning Day arrived: the eleventh of April. Dressed in No.1 Dress (Blues), I met my parents en route to Chapel Square. We found a pew in the packed Chapel, as the Band played an entre tune. The Order of Service included the patriotic 'I vow to thee my Country', by Thaxted, and an excerpt from chapter six of Saint Paul's letter to the Ephesians, read by the Commandant. The highlight, however, was the anthem, 'Panis Angelicus' sung by Second Lieutenant S.M.Kingham, the Sash of Honour winner.

I rushed away to put on my white belt and boots and collected my rifle from the armoury, complete with shimmering bayonet. We marched as a Company for the last time, on to New College Square and formed up in front of the Academy Adjutant. With parents and friends watching, we marched up to Old College Square, in time to the music of the Band of the Gurkhas (2nd Kind Edward VII's·Own Gurkha Rifles), listening intently to the thud of the bass drum. The succession of drill movements was performed as rehearsed and we marched past the Saluting Dais, grimacing at the thought of the wind blowing hats all over the Parade Ground. The Princess Royal, then Princess Anne, carried out the inspection and made a superb speech, noting the presence on parade for the first time of the complete Company of Women's Royal Army Corps Officers and Officer Cadets. Stirring references were made welcoming the visitors to the Royal Military Academy of Officer Cadets from overseas and to the cold weather they had faced. Despite the apparent pointlessness of marching around the parade ground The Princess Royal pointed out that:

'The Parade is nonetheless an impressive way of saying 'I made it' and showing your already proud family and friends the public face of the discipline and teamwork that are essential to any soldier, and the Parade also demonstrates the successful completion of your course . . . (Sandhurst's) sense of continuity, which will be at its greatest when you Slow March up the steps of the Grand Entrance, when you might be particularly conscious of your many distinguished predecessors.'

Our attention was drawn to the Sandhurst motto 'Serve to Lead', displayed on our cap badges and we braced ourselves for the Academy Adjutant's imminent take-over.

Amongst the thin lines of the senior division, I marched up the Old

College steps in slow time to the tune of 'Auld Lang Syne', to hear the colour Sergeant's knowledgeable comment: 'This is not the end; this is just the beginning!' ricocheting between the stone columns.

Around the back of Old College we handed in our belts and boots — with the polish scraped off in a gesture of defiance — and gave our rifles over to members of the junior division, who had to clean them. I moved swiftly over to Colonel Watson's house, where my Parents had gone to rendezvous. We had to rush to Victory College to beat The Princess Royal, fortunately arriving in the nick of time! We had been briefed that being presented to a member of the Royal family could be an awe-inspiring experience, but The Princess Royal seemed aware of this and put us all at ease within seconds of her arrival. I was presented alongside my parents, in the Royal Scots (The Royal Regiment) group as The Princess Royal was our Colonel-in-Chief. The other groups were made up of Officers and Officer Cadets in Princess Anne's other Regiments, prize winners and foreign dignitaries. As rehearsed, we filtered out of the lounge to arrive in the Dining Room before the Princess, standing to attention as she walked in towards the Prize Winners table. The Sovereign's Parade Luncheon was a gastronomic delight, worthy of any five star hotel, washed down with a St. Johanner Abbey Kabinett wine. It lasted for two hours which was just enough time to drive the Parade chill away!

I spent the remnants of the afternoon handing the few remaining articles of uniform in, before changing for the Commissioning Ball. My parents had organised a reception at the Frimley Hall Hotel for my guests so dinner was yet another mouth-watering meal. There was a ration of four Ball tickets per person, but many Officer Cadets only invited their girlfriends and it was not difficult to buy an extra allocation. I had managed to muster fourteen of my best friends, including my brother Tom and sister Tibi. Alice and Malcolm Liddell-Grainger were in fine fettle after a week of festivities in London, but could not be more adventurous than Romayne Craig and Christopher Fowler, who had, like my family, survived the thick traffic from Scotland! We were not the largest party, but we made up for our absent friends through determined festivity.

Nobody can give a party like the Army. And the Commissioning Ball (Sandhurst Ball) is the best of all the Army has to offer. There's a tremendous amount of energy and organisation which goes into each aspect of the entertainment, from the three marquees with adjoining corridors to the 'bucking broncho'; from the fair to the fireworks display. My Commissioning Ball was no exception. Wearing my Regimental Mess Dress for the first time, I arrived at the Ball in one of a convoy of friends' cars. We established ourselves at our pre-designated table and sped in different directions to an assortment of champagne bars. The top discos go out of their way to obtain a Commissioning Ball contract, which gives them

Alice Liddell-Grainger and Francis Salvesen at The Commissioning Ball.

incredible kudos, as well as 'street credibility' so we were not disappointed in our expectations of popular boppy music. Moving through from the main Jazz Hall, in the converted gymnasium, we found a selection of discos, complete with laser shows and videos, ending up at the fair, where waltzers were duly set in motion. We returned to the main dancefloor at midnight, just in time to hear the fanfare, marking the transformation of Officer Cadets to Officers. We bought some more champagne and, in a crowd of red, tartan and gold uniforms and multicoloured taffeta strode outside to the fireworks display. Dana Shaul and Alice Liddell-Grainger removed the black tape on my shoulders, with tremendous glee, revealing the pips underneath: I had become an Officer.

We continued partying until dawn, when exhaustion overcame us and we retired to our accommodation. As Peter Townend put it in 'Tatler',

'Having elegantly passed out in the presence of Her Majesty's Representative . . . 250 male and female Sandhurst graduates celebrated their release from the discipline of their course at the Commissioning Ball. Festivities temporarily ceased as midnight struck and, in a frenzy of champagne-spraying, the novice Second Lieutenants ripped the covering from their pips to reveal, bar mitzvah style, their new rank. At 6 a.m. those who smeared it cleared it, as, in traditional fashion, the soldiers cleaned up their own mess before marching off to their respective regiments.'

The metamorphosis was complete!

The author by Staff Sergeant A S Pring.

POET'S CORNER

Drill

It's fun to be out doing drill,
exotically dressed for the kill
like boxers going in for a mill
— the theory makes me quite ill!

'It's the Meaning of Life', I've been told,
though the story is not, as yet, sold.
It's disciplined, ornate and bold
— but rather inclined to be cold!

Formed up on The Square looking blue
like animals caged in a zoo,
erect to be lynched in the coup
or flung in the Show Parade queue.

When inspected we stand up quite straight
and announce our "All Present" state,
then await in intensive debate
for the terrible Show Parade fate.

The Platoon march to Old College Square
with a pride and a soldierly flair
marching on past the adjutants stare
and escaping his burst of hot air.

We march in Divisions of three
or in Columns, in two's, so they see
from the Stands how we arch to be free
of the dregs of . . . continuity.

There's a reason I cannot express
why we all hate our Number One Dress,
but when it turns out in a mess
The adjutant likes it much less!

91

Colour Sergeant P. Thomson S.G.

'Colour' Thomson is a man of war
who rests upon his grins.
He makes us drill and drill some more
to vanquish all our sins.

He studies all our movements
in a manner quite obscure
and when we think we've had enough
he drills us 'till we're sure.

He shouts at us: 'You LUNATICS!'
which may seem very terse —
but then again 'You LUNATICS!'
could well be something worse!

And when we're not parading
like Scots Guardsmen in disguise,
we're run to far horizons
to open up our eyes.

He bicycles to Tennis,
betting litres by the Gill.
He plays to adulation
and enthusiastic skill.

And when he thinks he's won a point
He'll jump for joy and yell
so when I say 'The ball was out!'
He'll say 'You go to Hell!'

Of course we see him late at night
when bull(y)ing boots together:
He shouts 'You Clot! You Lunatic!
You've bulled them to the leather!'

The moral of this awful prose
needs microscope-like glasses:
Don't give your boots the bull all night,
just polish all the brasses!

92

Mr. Ensign and his Parrot

I have been asked to write a verse
Describing in a manner terse
The difference that lies between
Our good host and his parrot green.

Our host is dressed in colours mellow
Not like the bird in green and yellow.
While parrots live in noisy ranks
In trees, our host likes quiet banks.
The parrot's beak is sharp and stark —
Our host need neither bite nor bark,
But chooses words, nor ever dreams
(Unlike the bird) of senseless screams.
For quite unlike the parrots grey
This bird has nothing good to say
And Mr. Ensign's conversation
Is worthy of all commendation.

To differentiate the two
I shortly point a way to you:
When you their signs of wisdom seek
One speaks, the other does not speak.

EPILOGUE

FRANCIS SALVESEN has written an interesting, informative and enjoyable book which should be of real help, not only to those who are fortunate enough to pass out of Sandhurst, but also to those who 'wonder what it is all like'; and many will be grateful for what he has written.

I have to add with extra pleasure and delight the debt that he has expressed to the late Donald Hankey whose Essays written during the first World War, and which I edited some years ago*, are as fresh today as they were when they were first published in the *Spectator* under the name of 'A Student in Arms'.

I have had the pleasure of knowing Francis Salvesen during all his schooldays at Cargilfield and Fettes College, and then through his time at Sandhurst; and I had the privilege of preaching in the lovely Chapel there and on quite a number of occasions during the time of such distinguished Commandants as Generals Gordon Lennox, John Mogg and Peter Hunt — all living examples of all that is meant by the often misunderstood expression of 'an officer and a gentleman'.

In an instructive, informal and sometimes amusing way Francis has shown how these qualities have still survived. The best commendation for this book would surely be that Donald Hankey himself would have approved and enjoyed what Francis has so ably written; and I am sure that many will be most grateful for this — and not only those who pass through Sandhurst.

He starts by quoting Donald Hankey's tribute to his Company Commander whom he called 'The Beloved Captain'. In the Foreword commending 'The Beloved Captain' Field-Marshal Sir James Cassels wrote . . . "The papers in this book are as young and relevant as when they were written. They are of priceless value to lead us in every walk of life and in any age".

*The Beloved Captain (Geoffrey Bles)

94

So I will finish with this short commendation and introduction with some words Donald Hankey wrote to the Beloved Captain's mother, Mrs. Hardy, when writing about her son. "What I want to say is simply that he had won the heart of every man from the roughest pitboy to the gentleman ranker, and that every one of us was proud to be commanded by him . . . Those who knew him will never forget him, he will always live in our memory as the ideal officer, a prince among men".

The picture of the ideal officer still remains, and it is the seeking after that prize that makes Sandhurst still what it is.

Ronald Selby Wright

The Queen's House,
Moray Place,
Edinburgh.
Autumn 1989

ABOUT THE AUTHOR

Francis Salvesen lined himself up for a military career at the tender age of fourteen, when he joined the Combined Cadet Force at Fettes College, Edinburgh. A year later, in 1982 he had completed an Outward Bound course in the Lake District and the Cadet Leadership Course at Frimley Park.

At the age of sixteen, Francis competed for an Army Scholarship at the Royal Military Academy Sandhurst and won the prize for 'character' on the United Kingdom Land Forces Cadet Leadership Course. He had already been made a junior N.C.O. in the cadets and passed a basic parachuting course.

He left Fettes in 1984 with a university complement of 'O' and 'A'levels, the bronze, silver and gold awards from the Duke of Edinburgh's Award scheme and a variety of outside interests, in the cadet rank of Colour Sergeant.

He was granted an 'O' type Commission in the Scottish Division, and, on discharge as a private soldier his military conduct was described as 'Exemplary'. He passed the Regular Commissions Board in December 1984 and entered the Royal Military Academy the following year.

On 11th April 1986 Francis Salvesen was commissioned into the Royal Scots (the Royal Regiment) in the rank of Second Lieutenant.

In 1988 he left the Army to study 'International Relations' at London School of Economics.

In 1989 Francis Salvesen won the British Council for Defence Information Award and represented Britain at the International Conference on National Security in Kiel, West Germany.